## Born to Be Wild

She is the Wild Girl.

We call her that because, like our natural wilderness,
she follows her own laws.

She is part of all of us, no matter what our age or sex.

She is freedom and joy, love of the quest and of movement.

She is creativity and serenity.

She is springtime, full of potential and energy.

She is the seed and the sprout, bursting with life.

She is the path through the forest,
and she is the forest itself.

## About the Author

Patricia Monaghan is one of the pioneers of the contemporary goddess movement. Her classic encyclopedia *The New Book of Goddesses & Heroines* remains the single most definitive source for information about the world's goddesses. She is a faculty member of the School for New Learning at DePaul University in Chicago, where she teaches science and literature. Visit her *Wild Girls* website at www.altogether.com/wildgirls/

## To Write to the Author

If you wish to contact the author or would like more information about this book, please write to the author in care of Llewellyn Worldwide and we will forward your request. Both the author and publisher appreciate hearing from you and learning of your enjoyment of this book and how it has helped you. Llewellyn Worldwide cannot guarantee that every letter written to the author can be answered, but all will be forwarded. Please write to:

Patricia Monaghan
℅ Llewellyn Worldwide
P.O. Box 64383, Dept. 1-56718-442-1
St. Paul, MN 55164-0383, U.S.A.

Please enclose a self-addressed stamped envelope for reply,
or $1.00 to cover costs. If outside U.S.A., enclose
international postal reply coupon.

Many of Llewellyn's authors have websites with additional information and resources. For more information, please visit our website at:

http://www.llewellyn.com

# The Path of the Young Goddess

## Patricia Mona[ghan]

2001
Llewellyn Publications
St. Paul, Minnesota 55164-0383, U.S.A.

First Edition
First Printing, 2001

Book design and editing by Rebecca Zins
Cover art ©2001 by Kris Waldherr
Cover design by Anne Marie Garrison

"Beyond the Turtle Ocean, Above the Western Sky" has also appeared in *Daughters of Nyx*, a magazine edited by Kim Antieau, in 1994.

"An Old Song, Bravely Sung" was published in *Magical Gardens* (Llewellyn, 1997) as "Sabulana, A Gardening Heroine."

Music on pages 164–166 from *Songs For Earthlings*, edited by Julie Forest Middleton. Published by Emerald Earth Publishing (www.EmeraldEarth.net) ©1998.

**Library of Congress Cataloging-in-Publication Data**
Monaghan, Patricia.
    Wild girls : the path of the young goddess / Patricia Monaghan.
      p.   cm.
    Includes bibiographical references and index.
    ISBN 1-56718-442-1
    1. Goddess religion.   2. Goddesses—juvenile stories.   I. Title: Wild girls. II. Title.

BL473.5 .M675 2001
291.2'114—dc21                          00-067007

Llewellyn Publications
A Division of Llewellyn Worldwide, Ltd.
P.O. Box 64383, Dept. 1-56718-442-1
St. Paul, MN 55164-0383, U.S.A.
www.llewellyn.com

 Printed in the United States of America on recycled paper

# Other Books by Patricia Monaghan

*Meditation: The Complete Guide* (with Eleanor Vierick)
(New World Library, 1999)

*The Goddess Path*
(Llewellyn, 1999)

*The Goddess Companion*
(Llewellyn, 1999)

*The Office Oracle*
(Llewellyn, 1999)

*The New Book of Goddesses & Heroines*
(Llewellyn, 1997)

*Magical Gardens*
(Llewellyn, 1997)

*O Mother Sun*
(The Crossing Press, 1994)

*Seasons of the Witch* (poetry)
(Delphi Press, 1992)

*Winterburning* (poetry)
(Fireweed Press, 1990)

For Paula and Barbara

*Wild Girl friends*

# Contents

## 5: White Shoulders, White Wings . . . 67
### *The Story of Finola*

## 6: Who Brought Endless Winter to the Land? . . . 83
### *The Story of Wakanee*

## 9: Beyond the Turtle Ocean, Above the Western Sky . . . 131
### *The Story of Pali Kongju*

## 10: An Old Song, Bravely Sung . . . 153
### *The Story of Sabulana*

# Introduction

## The Path of the Young Goddess

Once, ages ago, people pictured divinity as feminine, as a goddess. Serving that goddess were those like her: women priests.

Then, for more years than we can count, the goddess seemed to disappear. There were no marble statues of womanly power and strength to inspire human women. Women no longer presided at religious rituals. We still talked about Mother Nature, but she was no longer seen as divine.

Today, the goddess has been rediscovered, and women are again her priestesses. Today, hundreds and even thousands of people lift their voices in song and move together in dance, honoring the Earth that sustains our lives. Small groups gather to light candles and call upon her. And individual girls and women, men and boys, place flowers before images of the goddess and bow their heads in silent, heartfelt prayer.

You are part of the goddess revival if you have ever sensed the power of earth and sky in their beautiful daily dance with each other. You are part of the revival if you have watched, with love and admiration, the way a woman moves in strength and power. You are part of the revival if you have found—or even suspected—that within yourself you hold some of the ancient power of the feminine.

The goddess was honored whenever her stories were told. By learning the myths of the goddess, this book offers you a chance to join in that ancient form of worship. Naming her many names, knowing her many faces, acknowledging that she has never truly left us—these are the first steps on the path of the young goddess, the Wild Girl who lives within us and within our world still.

## Religions of the Earth

There has never been only one religion of the goddess. Every continent, every culture, had its own vision of the way the divine feminine should be pictured. Each culture pictured her as one of their own. She was black in Africa, blonde in Scandinavia, round-faced in Japan, dark-eyed in India. For the goddess was the essence of woman's strength and beauty to each one of her daughters, so she had to look like them. When ancient women looked at their goddess, they saw themselves.

The goddess is shown in such variety for another reason: because she is the Earth, and the Earth's features vary dramatically from region to region. The desert and the rainforest are as different as the goddesses of those lands. Mother Nature is not one, but many: the goddess of glaciers and snow, the goddess of the ocean, the goddess of forest, the goddess of desert sand.

Perhaps the goddess has been reborn in the hearts and minds of her children now because our world itself is threatened. Global pollution has killed many species in recent times and threatens many more. Glaciers in the Arctic retreat, melting away. Salmon no longer return to spawning streams to hatch new generations. The affluence and comfort of modern life has its cost: the depletion of our natural environment. The goddess has come to life again at a moment when we still have the chance to learn to be good citizens of our Earth—good children to our Mother.

## The Wild Girl: One of Her Many Faces

Although we speak of her as Mother Earth, the goddess is not only seen as a full-grown woman caring for her children. Just as each woman passes through different ages in her journey through life, the goddess is seen as a young woman, a woman in the prime of her life, a middle-aged woman, an old woman, and an ancient crone with more years than we can count. Sometimes the same goddess appears at various ages; at other times, different goddesses represent the different chronological moments of a woman's life.

Many contemporary goddess writers refer to the goddess as Maiden, Mother, and Crone. This triple goddess is found in some cultures, but not in all; where she is found, she is not always of distinctly different ages. For instance the Celts, ancestors to the Irish and Scots and Welsh of today, showed the goddess as three mothers, all apparently the same age. Other cultures showed the goddess in multiples rather than trinities, as with the Scandinavian Valkyries, a mob of fighting women, or the Greek Sirens, those seductive mermaids. Although the definition of the goddess as Maiden, Mother, and Crone is common today, it is only one way of sorting through the great variety of goddess images.

In this book, we will examine one image of the goddess that is found in many cultures: the young goddess. She is not necessarily a Maiden or virgin, for she may have engaged in sexual activity, by her own initiative or without her consent. Her age varies: sometimes she is ten, sometimes fifteen, sometimes twenty. She usually lives with her family, but sometimes she is alone in the wilderness. She can be found in every continent, among people of every color and race.

What is consistent about this goddess image is that it represents the questing, adventuresome part of a woman's soul. This goddess is always free to move and explore, to follow her own heart. This does not mean she denies family responsibilities or fails to care for others—in fact, hers is among the most loving and giving, even heroic, of goddess images. But even in her heroism, she is motivated by her own drives and desires.

She is the Wild Girl. We call her that because, like natural wilderness, she follows her own laws. She is part of all of us, no matter what our age or sex. Men, women, girls, and boys can all find a part of the Wild Girl within them. She is freedom and joy, love of the quest and of movement. She is creativity and serenity. She is springtime, full of potential and energy. She is the seed and the sprout, bursting with life. She is the path through the forest, and she is the forest itself.

The stories in this book have been collected from many sources and represent only some of the visions of the Wild Girl found throughout the world. Each of the stories is followed by commentary on the story's meanings and by activities to further explore these meanings. The stories may suggest other ideas and activities to you. Follow them, for this book is meant to inspire, not to limit, your adventures with your Wild Girl.

While this book is written especially for young women who are following the Wild Girl path to the goddess, older women and men can also enjoy and benefit from knowing her. In our dreams, in our souls, we can be any age and any gender. Mature women all have within themselves a memory of the girl they were; this book can help them get in touch with that energy and power. It may also help them to become more appreciative of the special struggles of young women—their daughters, granddaughters, students, employees—as well. Similarly, men and boys can benefit from getting in touch with their own inner femininity. In addition, following the path of the Wild Girl can help men understand the feelings and needs of the women and girls in their lives.

## Honoring the Goddess by Yourself

The path of the Wild Girl is not a passive one. It does not mean that you will just read this book, put it aside, and move on to another. It is an active encounter with yourself and with the great spiritual traditions of which the Wild Girl is a part. We honor the goddess through activities that express our respect and love for her and for ourselves. These activities form the basis of the spiritual practice of goddess religion.

Unlike religions that are based in churches with established hierarchies and liturgies, the religion of the goddess is an endlessly changing and evolving one. You can serve as your own priestess, creating or locating appropriate rituals to her. It is not necessary to have a group to follow the Wild Girl path. If you are a beginner and don't know of anyone else who is interested in this subject, create your own practice that includes meditation, creative efforts, and study. You may later meet others with whom you wish to share your spiritual experience. But the Wild Girl is herself often solitary, and she is well served by solitary efforts to connect with her energy.

## Honoring the Goddess with Others

Joining with a group to engage in spiritual searching is a powerful, though sometimes difficult, experience. It is powerful because the efforts of a group can enhance the effects of a ritual or creative exploration, and difficult because differing levels of skill and energy, insecurities and fears can create as much turmoil in a spiritual circle as in any other organization.

A Wild Girls' Circle, however, can become one of your most enriching spiritual experiences. The exercises in this book are designed to give you a sequence of activities to share; the twelve chapters provide a structure for a year of activities with a group. Chapter 13 offers information about how to create a Wild Girls' Circle, as well as suggestions for handling conflict and difficulty. You do not need dozens of friends to create your first Wild Girls' Circle. Two or three are enough. Every time you gather, you will know that, around the world, thousands and thousands of others are gathering too, adding their voices to the great and growing chorus that is calling the goddess back to the world today.

· · ·

# 1

# *Daughter of Nature, World Creator*

## Finland

Imagine a time before time was born. Imagine a time when no sun lit the colorless sky. When no moon shone silver on the dark sea. When no bird sang in a forest, no horse ran through long grasses, no bear slept in its cold cave.

Imagine a time when there was no air, no water, no earth. No life, no birth, no music. In all the universe, only three things existed. There was a river, in which flowed a swirling mix of possibility. There was space, blank and black and without even a single star.

And there was a girl.

The river was the power of movement in the universe. Space was the power of stillness. And the girl was their daughter.

Her name was Luonnotar, child of nature. She lived alone, with no sisters, no friends, no companions. There was nowhere for her to walk, so she did not walk; nowhere for her to run, so she did not run. She did nothing but rest on the stillness of space, watching the river glide into endlessness.

There is no name for what Luonnotar did. You cannot say that she was sleeping. To sleep means to dream, and to dream means to dream about something. But nothing had ever happened in all the endlessness that Luonnotar remembered, and dreams cannot be spun of nothingness.

But she was not truly awake. That would mean movement, and talk, and song, and pain. Luonnotar had nothing to say, nothing to sing, because nothing had ever happened to speak or sing about. Luonnotar felt no pain. But she felt no joy either. She simply floated, and watched, and waited.

Then one day—if there can be days where there is no time— something changed.

Something tightened in Luonnotar's chest. It felt as though her heart were bruised and hurting. She lay, floating on space near the endless river, wondering at this sensation. In the eternity of time- lessness, she realized—more slowly than you can imagine—that she was feeling something.

She felt desire. She felt emptiness. Into that emptiness flowed a river of yearning, want, longing.

What did she desire? Nothing had ever happened in the universe, so Luonnotar could not recognize that she yearned for action. Nothing had ever changed, so she could not know that she yearned for change.

But after that moment, as Luonnotar rested in cold space watching the black river flowing around her, she did so differently.

Slowly—more slowly than you can imagine—an idea came to Luonnotar. There had never been an idea in the universe before, so it took a long time to grow. After that immeasurable time, when her idea was full and ready, Luonnotar felt it rise like the first sun of thought. When it shone bright and strong in her mind, she acted.

Luonnotar dived from space into the great river.

It took but a moment. Then she was on the surface of the river. It was endlessly deep, but Luonnotar did not sink. Floating on her back, she looked up at the space from which she had leapt. There was no light there, no brilliant star nor radiant moon nor beaming sun. There was only emptiness and perfect stillness.

Luonnotar rested again, drifting through the universe on the waves of the river that flowed beneath space. She traveled vast distances, but it was as though she remained still. For everywhere, everything looked the same. There was still only a river, space, and a girl.

But no action, however small, is without effect. Everything in the universe is connected. Luonnotar's plunge had changed everything, forever. It took endless time for the change to reveal itself, but finally, something happened.

A duck swam up to Luonnotar.

A duck, in the whole empty universe where there had been only one being. How had this come to be, that there were now two?

It happened because Luonnotar moved. When she did, she shifted the axis of the universe. In her yearning for change, the girl had created a new world, a world in which a duck could exist.

Luonnotar lay very still. The tiny duck swam around and around, looking at the floating girl. Then she climbed onto Luonnotar's knee and sat down. The duck sat there calmly, out of the cold of the great river, upon the warm knee of the girl.

Then something else happened, something so beautiful that Luonnotar could not believe her eyes.

The duck laid three little eggs on her knee.

Luonnotar's knee was the only warm, dry spot in all the universe. It was the only place where the future could hatch.

Luonnotar lay very, very still.

She willed herself not to move in even the slightest way. The duck sat on her clutch of eggs, and the eggs grew warmer and warmer. The future, in all its sparkling variety, drew nearer and nearer.

Luonnotar yearned for that future. She yearned so much that the dull pain returned to her heart. But she ignored it. Her skin prickled from the heat, the feathers, and the tiny scratches of the duck's webbed feet. But she ignored that, too. The future was at stake, and she wanted to protect it. So day after day she floated, perfectly still. The duck sat upon the eggs, the eggs sat upon the girl's knee, and the girl floated upon the river of heaven.

Then, suddenly, the duck shifted her position. Her tail feathers tickled Luonnotar's skin. Luonnotar's knee twitched.

She did not mean to. It happened beyond her control. And it was not much: just a tiny twitch. But it was enough.

Luonnotar watched in horror as the precious eggs rolled off her knee into the cosmic river.

What had she done? The only task of her entire existence, and she had failed! Had she ruined everything? Luonnotar watched the eggs crash into the waves. She feared they would sink forever out of sight. She feared that the future would be lost in the black river of time.

Instead, the eggs broke open.

Marvels poured forth. The yolks joined together, forming a yellow ball, and rose shining into the sky. The whites joined together and formed the silver moon. The bits of shell sparkled and drifted upward until they shone down as the countless stars. In the blankness of space, where Luonnotar had seen nothing but emptiness for so long, light appeared.

It was magic. And Luonnotar, from whose yearning these marvels were born, was transformed. She dived beneath the surface of the heavenly river. Down, down she dived. Something was there. She could feel it calling to her.

There it was! Luonnotar spied a bit of mud in the darkness beneath the river. She grabbed some in her hand and swam to the surface. There she floated on her back, forming the mud into a cone upon her belly. When she placed it carefully on the river's surface, it rose up into a mountain.

She dived again, and again, and again. Each time she returned with a handful of mud, she created something new. One time it was an island, another time a forest-swept valley. Furiously, joyously, Luonnotar worked. She built peninsulas and continents, high peaks and fertile plains. She gouged rivers into the land and scooped out lakes.

Overhead, inspired by Luonnotar's creativity, the little stars assembled themselves into signs and designs. The moon learned how to show its changeful face to the new earth. The bright, beaming sun learned to rise and set, dividing endless time into days.

As Luonnotar built the land, it burst into bloom. Red flowers trumpeted from vines. Grasses waved softly in the new wind. Great forests rose, and tiny flowers sprang from hard, gray rocks.

And then the animals appeared, children of the new earth. Birds filled the forest with song. Horses ran upon the waving grasses. In mountain caves, bears made their cold dens. Monkeys chattered in the huge trees of the jungles. Whales plunged down, deep, deep, into the chilly ocean waters. Over great snowy peaks, eagles wheeled and soared.

Tired at last, the creator sat down upon a high mountain. Luonnotar looked up at the brilliant sky. She looked around at the green earth. She looked at the dark blue waters sparkling in the new sun.

She looked at all that she had made, and she knew that it was good.

• • •

## Goddesses of Finland

The story of Luonnotar, the girl who created the world, was told for countless generations by the Finnish people. Their land is in subarctic Europe—in Scandinavia, the armlike peninsula above Germany. But the Finns are not related to their neighbors, the Swedish and Norwegian peoples. They speak a different language, one only related to a few other languages in the world. Their gods and goddesses are different as well.

At the fireside on dark winter nights a hundred years ago, you could hear Luonnotar's story. The speaker might be an old woman who rocked and spun yarn as she unreeled the tale. It might be an old man, wrapped in an embroidered cloak and leaning on his carved staff. It might be a girl like Luonnotar, practicing a story that, after many years and countless tellings, she would know by heart. These storytellers also told tales of the sun goddess Paivatar, the girl who sat on the end of the rainbow, spinning light. They told about Meilikki, the Wild Girl of the woodlands, who adopted orphaned bear cubs and nursed them as her children.

They told of fiercer goddesses too. There was Louhi, the winter queen, so powerful she once stole the sun right out of the sky. There was weird Ovda who tickled travelers to death if they got lost in the forest. There was the most fearful one: Tuonetar, queen of death, who lived seven days' walk away from wherever you were, in a dark forest beyond a black river.

In those days, there was no entertainment other than the telling of stories, the singing of songs, and the playing of games. The old stories were told time after time after time. There were no books, but the teller spoke each word exactly as she had learned it. The stories we have today of the goddess in Finland are hundreds, possibly thousands, of years old, kept alive by these continual retellings.

Finland was distant from the growing cities of Europe, but eventually even it began to change. People who had lived for centuries like their ancestors began to forget the old ways. It is possible that the stories of Luonnotar and her sister goddesses would have been entirely lost but for the work of one man. A hundred years ago, Elias Lonnrot traveled from town to town, collecting the ancient stories of his people. He compiled them into a great collection called *The Kalevala*. Written in poetry, the old tales give us a sense of the spirit and imagination of the Finnish people who had created them and had, for so many years, kept the tales of Luonnotar and her sister goddesses alive in the winter darkness.

## Creativity and Sacred Space

Creativity is everywhere. At this instant across the world, billions of people are asleep, their minds dreaming up wild stories without an ounce of effort. Every one of those people will spend the night creating stories—unique, unrepeatable stories—sometimes funny, sometimes terrifying. Tonight you, too, will lie down and spend hours inventing stories . . . and the next night, and the next, for year after year after year.

As our dreams show, creativity is an effortless part of our lives. There is no person on earth who is not creative. But often we are discouraged by others from acknowledging that true, creative self. Thus the first step for anyone on the Wild Girl path is to get in touch with inner creativity by designing a sacred space for meditation, ritual, and self-expression.

In this, we act like the goddess, for her first action was to create the world. There are many stories, from many countries, that reveal the same secret wisdom: that the primary creative act of the feminine is to make a beautiful world out of nothing but space and time. Luonnotar is just one of dozens of creator goddesses who start with nothing and end with a world of miraculous beauty and plentiful life.

Each of us needs to create a world like that for ourselves, a private space where we will be safe and secure, a place for our creativity and passion. A place where we will never be mocked, where our hearts will never be broken, where all the colors and shapes and patterns sing to us of beauty.

Creating such sacred space is the first step in establishing your spiritual practice. Without a place into which you can retreat to regroup and restore yourself, you will find your energy constantly depleted and drained. Imagine what happens when you leave a car's headlights on overnight: next morning, the battery is dead. Sacred space is like a battery charger. When we plug into the healing energy of such a space, we are renewed.

This energy is not mysterious or strange or dangerous. It is a life force that flows around us like the great cosmic river on which Luonnotar floated. It is always around us, holding us up and sustaining us, as it did for the girl creator. But in the busy rush of everyday life, we can lose connection with that sustaining force. Being in sacred space reconnects us.

There are many famous sacred spaces on earth, places like Stonehenge in England and the pyramids in Egypt, to which pilgrims travel to restore their energy and balance. But you don't need to travel across the world to visit a sacred space. You can create sacred space whenever and wherever you wish.

You do not need much room. You can create your sacred space in a corner, if that is all you have. Purifying the space of negative associations, arranging it in a creatively pleasing way, and using it for ritual or meditation: these are the ways space is made sacred. We will cover the first parts of this process in this chapter, the last part in chapter 2.

If you have your own bedroom, that is the ideal place to create your secret, sacred space. A room entirely of one's own—no matter how small—is a treasure and a privilege. Only a tiny percentage of the world's population has access to such private space. In such a room, we can close the door against the world. We can hear our own music and explore our own joy. Of course, just having a door to close does not guarantee that a room will be a safe haven. Others may violate our space without our permission. But it remains sacred because we can purify it of negative influences each time we enter it.

Purification is the first step in creating sacred space. Unlike Luonnotar, we do not usually begin with empty space. Instead, we usually face a litter of objects, every one of which has its own story. A seashell brought back from a favorite beach; a photo of a friend with whom we have argued. What different energies each thing has! When you hold the first, you feel the peaceful beauty and wild storminess of the seashore. Your body relaxes, your breath comes in deep, strong rhythms, your heart rate slows. But when you pick up the photograph, your heart races with anxiety. Angry thoughts flood your mind. You feel your muscles tighten as though you were about to fight or run away.

Even when we are not paying attention, the objects in our surroundings whisper their stories to us. In sacred space, each object murmurs of serenity and joy. The first step in creating sacred space, then, is examining the objects within it. You can choose to do this with your entire room, or only with the part you will designate as sacred. Once you have set the parameters of your space, begin your work. If something is broken, either fix it or give it away to someone who will. If something holds negative memories, find it a new home—or at least put it away where you do not see it constantly. Have nothing in your space that brings you pain.

Purifying the space of negative associations frees you to be creative within it. Examine the colors in your space and, if you have control over them, change them to suit your taste, using paint or wallpaper. If you cannot change the color of walls or carpet, you can still use drapes and colorful fabrics to create a place of beauty—your beauty, with every aspect rewarding your eye with pleasure.

If possible, separate the space you wish to use as your sacred center from that used for other tasks. While it is possible to move your altar objects every time you need to do homework, it can be disruptive to your inner serenity. Dirty clothes piled up beneath your altar will dissipate your spiritual energies. It is optimal to have designated space for your rituals, meditations, and creative expressions, even if your sacred space is small.

If you have no private space, you face a special challenge. Even more disruptive than junk beneath the altar is the disruption of another person who is ignorant of, or dismisses, your spiritual quest. Fighting constantly about the need to honor your sacred space can be worse than having none at all. Sometimes the "hide in plain sight" approach can work in such circumstances: create a sacred space that looks like an ordinary part of the room. Paint a goddess image on a scarf and lay it casually across a dresser. Put some special rocks in a little basket by the bedside, then put a candle next to it. Collect all the common-looking objects you can that have spiritual significance to you—books, knickknacks, and so forth—and arrange them in a way where their significance is known only to you.

Should you find your private space disrupted, take a few moments to restore it to order. As you do so, breathe deeply—anger causes us to breathe shallowly, which in turn makes us more angry—and imagine setting up an impenetrable wall between yourself and the offending party. Do this as often as necessary. Do not argue with the person who has disrupted your space; this offers them more power over you. Take back your own power by rebuilding your space, feeling your inner power as you do so.

It is sometimes impossible to find a place to create sacred space indoors, especially if others are continually disrespectful. In that case, look outside for a place you can use for your meditation and other spiritual practices. This can be difficult in cities where outdoor spaces are not advised for women alone, but it can also be difficult in less-urban areas where neighbors might be intrusive. Again, remember that your space need not be large. A corner in the yard is enough. Public land, such as that on a campus or in a park, is also sometimes an option, provided you use it during daylight hours or when otherwise protected from any possibility of being disturbed. Depending on your climate, seasons could limit your usage of an outdoor sacred space, but once a space is purified and used for spiritual purposes, you can re-create it within your mind when you need to.

If you are creating outdoor sacred space, become the steward of that part of the land. Do not let litter rest on the ground or allow other damage to be done. Do not disturb your plant and animal neighbors, either. Your sacred space is not a good place to put a bug zapper or to use toxic chemicals.

## Creating a Personal Altar

Once your sacred space, whether indoors or outdoors, has been purified, you are ready to build an altar there. An altar is nothing more than an arrangement of objects placed together creatively to evoke a special state of mind in the beholder. The arrangement of objects on the altar speaks to our deep mind, which learns in images rather than in words.

All altars are built with a purpose, but some have more general, and others more specific, focuses. A general altar is decorated with objects that evoke your ongoing spiritual quest; a specialized altar is built for a certain specific intention. A collection of goddess images is appropriate for a general altar; a stack of math books would be appropriate for an altar to help you do better in school.

Building an altar is your first creative act as an aspiring initiate of the goddess, as a follower of the Wild Girl. There is no recipe book for making an altar. Begin with your intention and move outward to its manifestation. Each girl's altar will be distinct and unique. For example, imagine that your intention is to become more self-confident physically. One person might put a silver charm of a tennis shoe on the altar to represent her aspiration to become more vigorous and athletic. Someone else might chose to put filmy scarves on the altar, like those used by Middle Eastern dancers. Only you can decide what objects should deck your altar.

For a general altar, include a representation of the goddess. This can be a picture or sculpture, or a natural symbol such as a flower or a rock. Represent as well the four elements: earth, air, fire, and water. Consider symbols of your heritage; ritual objects like candles; seasonal decorations; mementos of special times. Arrange these objects in a fashion you find pleasing. Renew the altar regularly by dusting and otherwise cleaning it.

For a more specialized altar, determine what your intention is. Remember that the objects on the altar are subliminal reminders to you of your intention, so spend some time clarifying what you really want. Do you really want to get into that prestigious school—or do you want respect from others? What good is an altar full of test-prep books if, once you get into the prestigious school, you still feel no one respects you? It may be far better to build an altar with photos of people who get the respect you want—with a photo of yourself right there in the center.

Once you have clarified your intention, look for items that symbolize it. Do not restrict your search: newspaper clippings can be part of an altar as much as a single red rose. A good way to begin this quest is through brainstorming. Write down everything that could represent what you want, even the silly or ridiculous things. Make a list of at least thirty items. Do not stop with a couple of ideas; keep pushing. Good ideas can hide under dull ones. Lift the lid, let the trite ideas out, and find the gold beneath.

You do not need to restrict yourself to one altar. Build many small ones: a little arrangement of flowers and crystals by your mirror to remind you of the beauty of the goddess within you; a statue of a goddess of art on your study table. Anything can be an altar if you choose. Remember: intention, purification, and ritual use are what defines an altar space.

# Where to Find Altar Objects

## *Natural Objects*

Any natural object is a good choice for your personal altar. Choose objects that help you visualize the energies that you would like to embody. If you are seeking to connect with the goddess's strength, try stones on your altar. If you are seeking joy, light objects like feathers and milkweed silk are appropriate.

Stones

Feathers

Flowers

Leaves

Shells of wild bird eggs (note: do not take birds' nests; many birds use the same nests every year or recycle them)

Water from streams and lakes

Tree branches and bits of wood

Shells

Crystals

## Goddess Images

The goddess may be seen as human or in another form. This means you have many options for your goddess image. Horse goddesses, for instance, can be symbolized by glass figurines or photographs of wild mustangs. You need not know the name of a goddess to use her image, although curiosity will probably lead you to search out her name and story. The further reading section at the back of the book provides information on where to find goddess images and books on the goddess. Purchasing a goddess image is not necessary. Find one in a book on mythology and copy her image, in painting or sketching or sculpture. Such a personalized goddess encourages your creative self.

Photographs

Paintings

Sculptures

Fabric painting

Embroidery

Collage

## Ritual Objects

Your meditations and private rituals (or rituals you share with your Wild Girl friends) may require tools. You need not keep them all on your altar continuously. Arrange whatever you place on your altar in keeping with your inner intention.

Salt

Water

Candles

Incense

Knife

## *Objects of Beauty*

Anything you find beautiful is appropriate for your altar. Remember you are speaking to your deep self, aligning your energies to gain your intention. Whatever speaks to you of beauty reflects the beauty of your soul.

Books of poetry

Photographs and paintings

Scarves and other fabrics

Lace and ribbons

Mirrors

Jewelry

Pieces of colored or stained glass

Silver candle holders

Crystal dishes

## *Personal Mementos*

There are times in your life when you feel in contact with the wild energy of the goddess. For many people, these moments occur in natural settings, in places of earth power. But they can occur in a crowded city as well, or even in our own home. An object that reminds you of such a moment is a powerful addition to your altar. Remember: your altar is not a scrapbook. Do not use it as a way to cling to the past. Only use objects that represent your future.

Photographs of important people

Postcards

Letters

Diaries

Antiques

Souvenirs of sacred places

## Activities for Creative Wild Girls

Make a play diary. Record in it what you remember of yourself as a child. How did you play? With whom did you play? What did you like to do? Why? Select one favorite activity from your childhood and do it once a week for a month. Then select another. Do this for at least four months.

Go for a half-hour walk. As you walk, pretend you do not know the names of anything you see. Look at everything. What surprises you? Invent new names for what you see. What do these new names tell you about the objects and about yourself?

Write a list of creative women you admire, including women you know personally and those you know by reputation. Put it on your altar for a week, then put it away. Do this once a month for a year. At the end of the year, take all your lists and see what names appear most frequently. What do those women have in common?

Make an inner wilderness collage. For a few weeks, look for photos and artwork in magazines that correspond to your creative inner self. When you have assembled enough, arrange them on a sheet of cardboard, creating the design of a landscape: a forest, a mountain scene, a lake, whatever expresses your inner wilderness. Cut out the images as carefully as possible, using only the most emotionally powerful parts. Glue the pieces onto the backing and put on your altar.

Begin a diary of your spiritual quest. In it, write experiences that seem unusual or magical. Do not use this diary to record everyday events. You will find more suggestions for your spiritual diary in chapter 9.

## 2

# *Until Every Living Thing Is Holy*

## China

**W**ithin each of us, a glowing light marks the place where our soul touches the universe. Those who never look within live in endless shadow, unaware of their soul's potential. Others dimly know of the light's existence but never feed it, so that it slowly gutters out. But some give energy to their inner light until it grows into a bonfire that illuminates the ages.

One such soul had lived many lives on this Earth, each increasingly holy. By the time this soul was born into the body of a girl named Miao Shin, the white fire burned strongly. It could have been that soul's last life on this Earth. But Miao Shin made a fateful decision, and we have all been blessed as a result.

Miao Shin's parents were a gentle, soft woman and a fierce, angry man. The girl had her mother's kindness. She loved wild plants and all the animals in the forest. She loved people, too, and found good in everyone.

But she also had her father's stubbornness.

When she was nine, Miao Shin went walking alone on a nearby mountain. There she met a hermit woman, very thin and almost hairless, whose eyes bulged out of her head. Most would have found her ugly, but Miao Shin saw the woman's inner beauty. She sat with the strange old woman as the sun set and darkness gathered. There, beside the old woman, Miao Shin felt at peace.

From that moment, Miao Shin knew she would become a hermit. Back home, she taught herself how to meditate. Each morning and evening, she sat on a porch facing the sun. She silenced the chattering of her mind. No more did she talk to herself about what dress to wear or how to braid her hair. Instead, silence filled her with its radiance.

In this way, she discovered her inner light.

Her father was not pleased. A hermit in the family! It was absurd, embarrassing. He scoffed at her spiritual quest. "She's nine!" he yelled at Miao Shin's mother. "Wait until she's fifteen! Then she'll want to marry!"

Miao Shin's father did not want his daughter to marry so that she might be happy, with a strong husband and sweet children. He thought only of himself. He wanted servants and gold. And his daughter, he had decided, would get them for him. Miao Shin's father had arranged for her to marry a man of great wealth, neither young nor handsome.

As the wedding day approached, Miao Shin asked no questions about her bridegroom. She did not bother to be fitted for a wedding dress. She showed no interest in what flowers would deck the house. She simply sat in meditation, for hours and hours and hours, every day.

She was trying to find the place where her soul met the center of the universe. Sometimes she reached, in the white inner light, a deep calm. It did not last long. But Miao Shin knew that the light was growing stronger.

Her mother argued with her father. "She will not make a good wife," Miao Shin's gentle mother said. "Look at her. She is interested only in holiness. Do not force her to marry against her will."

But the father would not listen. A marriage had been arranged; a marriage there would be. No mere girl would humiliate him before his friends! No daughter of his was going to run off to become a hermit!

But his anger and entreaties led to nothing. The girl still sat in silence. So Miao Shin's father tried another approach: he sent her to a convent. The dull convent food and the company of dull nuns, he thought, would surely cure her of her delusion of holiness.

But Miao Shin loved the convent. At last she was with women like herself! They wore simple clothes and ate simple foods. For hours they sat together silently, searching for peace and illumination. For hours they chanted quiet prayers. It was all Miao Shin wanted. Her meditations grew deeper, more profound.

When her father heard that Miao Shin was thriving in the convent, he was furious. "Drag her from that convent!" he ordered his men, and they did so. "Lock her in that tower," he proclaimed, pointing to an ancient ruin near the road. And they did so.

In the tower, there was no one to talk to and only dry rice to eat. Miao Shin devoted herself to her discipline. Mornings she prayed facing the rising sun. Evenings she prayed facing the setting sun. In between, she meditated on the light. Soon she saw the bright truth behind the shadows of this life.

At last, Miao Shin's father saw the truth, too. He realized that everything he tried only made his daughter stronger in spirit. He realized that, even if he forced her to marry, she would never be a proper wife. If she were sent home by an angry husband, he would never get the gold he desired.

Flying into a rage, he ordered his soldiers to kill Miao Shin.

The soldiers, like everyone in the household, loved and respected the girl. But they feared her father more. So they took Miao Shin from the tower and led her out into the forest. They were silent, ashamed of what they were about to do.

Miao Shin knew why they trooped so somberly into the woods. She knew she was to be killed. And she knew it was her own father who had given the order. But she did not object. Instead, she walked quietly behind the soldiers, her thin wrists tied with heavy rope, knowing that there was a design behind all things.

The soldiers reached an open space in the trees. They drew their swords. Miao Shin took a deep breath, readying herself for her next life. The soldiers raised their swords, as one, into the air.

Suddenly a tiger bounded out of the woods. It was huge, bigger than any tiger ever seen. With a sweep of a long foreleg, the tiger knocked away the swords of the soldiers. Taking Miao Shin in its mouth, it ran through the forest until it reached a low mountain cave. There it dropped the girl on the rocky ground.

Miao Shin looked up at the huge jaws of the tiger. Being torn apart by the beast was even worse than being killed by a cold iron sword. But she breathed deeply and prepared again for death.

The tiger disappeared.

Miao Shin was alone in the dark cave. She looked around at the dripping wet walls. Then, without warning, the cave dissolved. Miao Shin floated like a feather in the wind.

She landed somewhere. It was a dark, dismal place, far worse than the mountainside cave. Before her, ghosts drifted like smoke. Above them, she saw a huge man, with flames darting out of his head and eyes. It was Yen Lo Wang, ruler of the dead.

She was in his realm. But had she died? She did not remember dying. Miao Shin touched her fingers to her face. No—her skin was warm, she still lived. Then why was she here?

Miao Shin looked around at the sad floating ghosts. Yen Lo Wang held them in his grasp. Trapped this way, they could never be reborn. They could never pay for their crimes nor seek enlightenment. Miao Shin realized she had come here to perform a holy work.

"Wang," she demanded of the god, "why do you hold these souls here in bondage? They must be born again on Earth to work off their evil deeds. Why keep them here in misery, where they can never reach salvation?"

The god scowled. Flames sprang like snakes from his head. The girl stood before him, shining like a saint. He wanted no saints here! He opened his mouth to bellow. He raised his hand to curse. But then a peace fall upon him such as he had never felt before.

Miao Shin stood before him, calmly meditating. Her inner light blazed around her. The ghosts, drawn to the radiance, drifted toward her. The god of death saw and knew he had no power over the holy girl.

"Take them," he said. He was not kind, but he was no longer angry. "Take them with you."

Miao Shin blessed the drifting ghosts. They drifted upward and disappeared. On Earth, they slipped into the bodies of newborn babies, ready to live again and to correct mistakes they had made in other lives.

Miao Shin blinked. Immediately she was back in the cave on the Earth's surface, where she had been carried by the divine tiger.

She sat down and began to meditate. She felt light rising in her like water in a glass filled under a waterfall. When the glass was almost full, she opened her eyes.

Before her stood the Buddha! His face was joyous and kind. "Miao Shin, you have attained enlightenment," he said, his voice full and serene. "You are very near to becoming a manifestation of all that is divine. But your father wants to stop you. So you must hide. Go to the holy island of Polata. There you will find the silence you need to become perfectly holy."

The girl nodded somberly. She was eager to be on with her task of further enlightenment.

"But first," the Buddha said, "you must eat this peach. It comes from the Garden of Heaven. You will be without hunger or thirst."

She ate the sweet, juicy peach and felt more satisfied than she had ever been before. A dragon appeared at the cave's door. Miao Shin mounted it and flew across the ocean to the island of Polata.

On the Isle of Polata, Miao Shin performed even more rigorous prayer and meditation. She rose before the sun and greeted it with prayer. She performed all her actions in the same spirit of worship. Whether she was cutting potatoes or building a fire, taking care of orphaned ducks or smelling a flower, Miao Shin brought to every moment a sense of the fullness and divinity of life. She had found peace at last.

After nine years, Miao Shin was even more holy than when she had arrived. One day she sat in meditation on her island, looking from a high hill out to sea. As she did so, she began to glow from within. Her body shone like gold. From within her soul, the beauty of her being was bursting through her flesh. She became a bodhisattva, a near-Buddha, a person of magical powers and utter kindness.

Far out at sea, she saw fishermen net a huge gasping fish. But it was no fish, as her inner eye could see: it was the son of the Dragon King of the Sea. The fishermen brought the big fish to market to be sold. Within a few hours, the prince would be cooked and eaten. But Miao Shin flew to the marketplace and purchased the writhing dragon prince. She took him to the sea, and there she set him loose.

In gratitude, his father gave Miao Shin the Night Brilliance Jewel, an ornament so beautiful it shone at night. The dragon king's granddaughter, Lung Nu, carried the jewel to Miao Shin. Recognizing the bodhisattva's greatness, the princess dedicated herself to Miao Shin's service and remained with her on the island.

During many years as bodhisattva, Miao Shin helped people wherever she could. She rescued drowning sailors, helped victims of bandits, provided food for the starving. She could see throughout the world, so she knew the pain of each homeless child. She could hear everything in the world, so she knew the soft sobs of each tired orphan. And she could fly, so she flew to the rescue of each of them.

With each action, she grew more holy. At last, she was strong and pure enough to return home. She knew she could never be free until she did so.

Her mother had long since died. But her father was still alive—her father, who had hindered her prayers and tried to kill her. When he saw his brilliant daughter, bursting with magical powers, he quivered in fear. "I am an old man," he sobbed. "Do not hurt me for what I have done to you."

Miao Shin comforted him. "I do not come to hurt, but to heal," she said. And then she showed him the tiny pearl of goodness still within him. She told him of the path to enlightenment. She stayed but a few hours and, in that time, she saved her father.

With that action, Miao Shin became as holy as a Buddha. She was on the verge of disappearing from this world forever, of passing into a place of eternal light and peace, of joining with the universe's deepest power. She felt that power surge within her and the outlines of her body begin to dissolve. But then, summoning all the force she had, she resisted.

"I do not wish it," she said to the universal light. "People are still unhappy. Everywhere I see misery and suffering. People starve, people fight each other in wars. Everyone is holy, but they do not yet know it."

The edges of her being grew more solid. She retreated from the space at which she had aimed through so many lives. She retreated from the perpetual calm and holiness that she had sought. "I wish," she said into the endlessness of space, "I wish to stay on Earth until every living thing is holy."

The divine force swept over her with a wave of love. She had given up Buddhahood in order to help others! Some small part of

23

her felt sad—all those lives of searching, and for what?—but the rest of her was swept away by the desire to do good.

She had the chance right away. Across the world, a small girl was crying. She had been beaten by a neighbor in the dark street. In her little room, the girl knelt and prayed.

"Kuan Yin Pu'sa," she prayed. The words had never been spoken before that moment. "O holy Kuan Yin."

At the instant of Miao Shin's decision, a new prayer had come into the minds of everyone on Earth. It was a prayer to a new Buddhist saint, a kind of goddess who had never before existed. For Miao Shin, the girl who sought goodness, had become Kuan Yin. Source of all mercy in the world, Kuan Yin would remain until everyone and everything on the Earth was saved.

Gathering her robes, Kuan Yin flew to the little girl's side.

• • •

# Goddesses of China

Buddhism is one of the world's great religions. Those who follow the path of the Buddha live in many lands: in India and Tibet, in Japan and China, in America. Like any belief held by millions of people, Buddhism and its practices vary greatly in various regions of the world. But a core belief, held by Buddhists around the world, is that some kind of meditation—turning inward, away from the noise of daily life—can lead us to truth.

Most, though not all, Buddhists believe that we are born again and again, living life after human life until we finally reach enlightenment. One who reaches enlightenment is called the Buddha, a name we frequently hear applied to the Indian prince Siddhartha, who became enlightened nearly two thousand years ago while sitting under a tree in meditation. But the statues that deck Buddhist temples are not statues of Siddhartha, because with enlightenment he ceased to be that man and became the Buddha in human form.

One who is nearly Buddha—who is close to reaching enlightenment—is called a bodhisattva. In ancient China, the girl Kuan Yin turned away from perfect enlightenment in order to help others. She remains one of the most beloved Buddhist saints, her image found in Chinese homes and businesses. She appears as a lovely young woman, draped in flowing garments, often holding a magical implement that shows her kindly nature.

Kuan Yin is often called a goddess, but that is not strictly true, as there are no goddesses in Buddhism—nor any gods, either. There is only the universal force of truth. But before Buddhism was brought to China by Indian travelers, the Chinese people had many goddesses. There was Chang-O, the moon goddess; Chih Nu, the weaving woman of heaven; Hsi-Ling Chih, the goddess who invented silk. Most important was Hsi Wang Mu, the Queen Mother of the West, in whose sacred palace lived the magical peach tree of eternal life.

Even after Buddhism became an important religion in China, these goddesses continued to be honored. For most of this century, Chinese people have been discouraged by their government from following their traditional religions, but prayers to Kuan Yin and other powerful feminine spirits are nonetheless still offered throughout the world.

## Learning to Meditate

Meditation is one of the world's most widespread spiritual practices. Virtually every region has its own tradition of meditation. Some are active, like drumming and dancing; some are very still, like breathing or sitting meditations. Some create a feeling of exuberance or intoxication, others of serenity and peace. What they all have in common is that they remove the mind from everyday concerns.

Buddhism often talks about "monkey mind" and "wild mind." Monkey mind is the way our mind works most of the time: like a chattering monkey, rushing from subject to subject, making lots of noise. You begin to think of a test at school; you worry that you aren't prepared; your mind begins to scream with anxieties until you feel like screaming yourself. It is as though your mind has a mind of its own!

In meditation, the first goal is to quiet the monkey mind, to get it to stop chattering and jumping around the cage. With enough practice, something else emerges: the wild mind. This is the mind freed of worries and everyday concerns—the mind as it was meant to be, free and spontaneous and wildly imaginative.

But getting from monkey mind to wild mind is not a quick journey. It may take years, in fact, before you can quiet the monkey when you choose. Even a beginning meditator, however, can calm down somewhat and begin to quiet the raging mind. But do not wait to try meditation until the mind is out of control. To gain the benefits of meditation, you need a regular, probably daily, practice.

The kind of meditation described in this chapter is the basic Buddhist form of sitting meditation. To start, find a comfortable place to sit. Advanced meditators usually sit on the floor, backs straight, upon a little pillow. But you may wish to start with your back supported by a chair or couch or wall. Rest your hands on your knees in a comfortable position.

Now breathe.

That's it. Just sit, and breathe. Do this for ten minutes.

It seems so simple, but in fact sitting meditation is very difficult. Your mind will wander. Your skin will itch. Your knees will get stiff. You will find, at first, that sitting for even a short time takes quite a bit of effort. Do not give up, however. The benefits are not felt the first time, or even the second or third. Take time to meditate daily, and you will notice that you are calmer when faced with a crisis. You have begun to calm the monkey mind.

Some teachers advise that you picture your mind as a blue sky. Whenever a thought appears, just watch it float across that sky like a puffy cloud. Do not attach other thoughts to it. Monkey mind does that: thought of the test leads to thought of the cute boy in class, which leads to thought of the awful outfit you were wearing last time you met, which leads to thoughts of not having anyone to go out with on the weekend, which leads to thoughts of never having a boyfriend, ever, ever, ever. . . .

It is so easy for monkey mind to start its chattering hysteria!

Instead, when you think of the test, just notice that you are thinking of the test. Do not pursue the thought. Do not comment on it, either positively or negatively. Just let it pass through you. Watch the cloud go across the blue sky. Do not try to hurry it along. It will pass, and the sky will be empty and blue again.

It is difficult to maintain such mental emptiness for long. Do not be surprised or discouraged if meditation seems difficult. There are rewards for persevering. After a few months, you will notice that you are calmer and happier. You will make decisions more easily. You will find it easier to talk to people because you are less controlled by your inner monkey.

And sometimes, in the midst of your meditation, you will become aware of wild mind. It is as though suddenly, in the clear blue of your inner sky, the sun shines in a blaze of light. Without the chattering distractions of monkey mind, your inner wilderness can be experienced in all its beauty.

# Making a Meditation Pillow

Many Buddhist meditation centers provide pillows for meditators, who sit on the floor with crossed legs. This provides physical comfort. It does something else as well: it is a signal to the body/mind that meditation is about to begin. For we are not separated into body, mind, and spirit. All are part of a unity. Therefore what affects the body also affects mind and soul. Your deepest self does not speak in words but in images. The pillow is a cue to the deeper self that it is time to quiet the monkey.

Making a meditation pillow will reinforce that message to your deepest self. Because many girls do not have sufficient sewing skills to make an entire pillow, these instructions are for decorating a premade pillow. However, if you can sew by hand or machine, making the entire pillow or re-covering an old pillow will be an even more rewarding project, for you will have more time to focus on your goal as you craft this creation.

To make a meditation pillow, start with a square purchased pillow in a plain fabric. The choice of color is up to you, though calming colors (blue, green, gray) are appropriate to your desire to calm the mind. The pillow should be small (8 x 8 or 10 x 10), but big enough for you to sit on comfortably.

In addition to the pillow, you will need a piece of felt fabric, some fabric glue, and some fabric paint in applicator jars. All are readily available at craft stores. You also need a piece of paper the same size as the pillow top, scissors, a compass, and some pins.

Using the compass, measure out a circle pattern on the paper. It should fit easily on the pillow top, allowing some room for decoration. Cut out the pattern with a scissors, then lay it on the felt. Cut carefully, making the edges even and neat.

Then lay the circle on the pillow. In doing so, you have created a mandala—a sacred shape comprised of a circle in a square. Using fabric glue, glue the circle carefully into the center of the square. Be sure to put enough glue near the edges to hold them down tightly. Wipe up any extra glue from around the edges as you work. Pressing from the center, make sure the circle lies smoothly on the pillow. Again, wipe up any glue that seeps out from the edges.

Let the pillow dry thoroughly. Check the fabric glue container to see how long you will need to wait before further decorating the pillow. In the meantime, draw a scale model of the pillow top on a piece of paper. Using geometrical shapes, determine how you will decorate the pillow. You could draw small triangles out from the circle to form a sunlike shape. You could draw a circle in the center of the felt, then radiating lines to the pillow corners. You can make your design as elaborate or as simple as you desire.

Once the pillow is dry and you are satisfied with your design, copy it onto the pillow using the fabric paints. (You could also embroider or otherwise stitch the design, in which case you should decorate the circle before attaching it to the pillow.) Using the applicators like pens, draw the designs onto the felt and the pillow surface. You may need to practice on scrap fabric before beginning the application, as in unsteady hands the paint can come out in heavy beads rather than crisp lines.

When the design has been copied, let it dry thoroughly before sitting on the pillow. Keep it near your altar or in another place where it does not get used for anything but meditation. Sit on your pillow whenever you meditate. Take it along when you spend the night away from home. It is a symbol of your spiritual quest, so care for it well.

## Many Types of Meditation

The meditation described in this chapter is only one kind, based in the spiritual traditions of Buddhism. There are many, many other kinds of meditation—almost all the religions of the world have their own form of it. In addition, many ordinary activities lend themselves well to meditation, to focusing the mind. You may wish to try some of these other forms.

### Eastern Traditions

Yoga: Consisting of postures derived from ancient Indian religion, yoga is a spiritual discipline requiring intense concentration and openness to illumination.

29

**Tai chi and qigong:** These Chinese meditations require movement and are sometimes used for physical healing. Both have spiritual beliefs at their core. While yoga is usually done on a mat on the floor, tai chi and qigong are usually done standing.

**Islamic meditations:** Dancing or whirling is a form of Islamic meditation. The nondenominational Dances of Universal Peace are derived from Islamic Sufi dancing; they involve singing simple songs while moving in meditation.

## Western Traditions

**Candle meditation:** Lighting a candle and observing its flickering flame while holding an image of spiritual transformation is a common neopagan meditation. It can result in self-hypnosis and should be used with care.

**Christian meditation/contemplative prayer:** Meditation is not restricted to non-Christian religions. Prayer, especially prayers repeated over and over again, is a form of meditation frequently used in Christian religions.

**Inspirational reading:** Many self-help programs rely upon a form of meditation that requires reading simple passages each day and reflecting on their meaning. Any book of spiritual value can be used.

# Activities for Meditative Wild Girls

Take a meditative walk. Select a place, indoors or outdoors, where you will be undisturbed and where there is nothing to collide with. Closing your eyes, walk as slowly as possible across the space, taking at least fifteen minutes to do so. Feel your heel leave the ground and your toes lift. Feel the muscles as they struggle to keep you upright. Feel the way your weight shifts as you put your foot down. Concentrate only on walking.

Find a picture of a Tibetan mandala or other sacred geometrical image. These can be found in art books or on cards in bookstores. Sitting quietly, let your eyes follow the patterns of the image for ten minutes. If thoughts disturb your observation, put them aside without developing them.

Select a short piece of orchestral music (one without words). Sitting quietly, with your eyes closed, listen to the music. Do not let thoughts intervene. If you feel a thought arise, think of it as a fish leaping out of the deep sea. Let it dive back in and leave the calmness unchanged.

Write nonstop for ten minutes. Do not correct any mistakes you make. Do not worry about spelling. Do not edit out anything. Let the words flow. When the ten minutes are up, do not read over what you have written. Tear up the page and throw it away.

Put on some music with a strong beat but no words. Cover your eyes with a scarf. Stand in the middle of the room and let the music fill you. When you feel that you are really listening to the music, not to your mind, begin to move. You do not need to move quickly. Just move, letting the music speak through you.

· · ·

# 3

# *Beauty Is Before Me, Behind Me, and Below Me*

## Navaho/Desert North America

**B**eauty came from the midst of war. It came from beneath the earth, from the realm of death. And it was brought to us by a girl.

That is what the Navaho of the great American desert say. This is how they tell the story:

Once there were two girls, born of the people of Gray Earth. Glispa and Tawa were sisters, children of the Rock House family. They lived in a dry land near the pueblos, those huge sandstone cities in the desert.

Young as they were, Glispa and Tawa had already seen war. For a long time, the Gray Earth people had been at war with the people of the pueblos. Young and old, man and woman, frail and healthy, all suffered and many died in the long conflict.

Each day the warriors fought, one against one, on the dry plain. Each night the warriors camped under the stars: at La Plata and Jemez, at Gray Mountain and Hard Flint. It was at Hard Flint that two ugly old warriors came to join the Navaho. From Wild Choke-cherry Patch came Bear Man, from Wide Rock came Big Snake. The young warriors ignored them, for they seemed too old to fight. But the young warriors were wrong.

One morning, as breakfast fires still smoked the sky, the warriors prepared for battle. The pueblo warriors were so fearful that just to look at them froze your bones, but the brave Navaho men won the day. That night they celebrated, each proving how many they had killed.

The one who had killed the first enemy would gain the most honor. Many laid claim. As the argument grew fierce, some of the warriors seized Glispa and her sister. "Whoever killed the first ones," they announced, "will get these girls for himself."

Right away the ugly old warriors came forward, each offering proof that he had killed the first dead. But the young warriors laughed. "These girls will not be given to them," the warriors agreed among themselves. Despite the proof, they wanted to keep the girls for younger men.

So the young men announced a contest for possession of the girls. First there was a shooting contest. And who pierced the center of the target, both at exactly the same instant? The two old men. So the young men repeated the contest. Again the old men won. A third contest was held, this time with contestants blindfolded. Again the old men shot the best shots.

A contest of distance shooting was held. The old men won it. Then there was backwards distance shooting. Again the old men won.

The warriors decided it was time for a war dance. All this time, Glispa and her sister had been held captive. But now, in the rush to gather drums and paint faces, they saw a chance for escape.

Silently they slipped their bonds and sneaked away. Silently they walked until they were safe in the scrubby forest.

There they smelled the strong, sweet odor of tobacco, the sacred herb used to bring visions. "Let's go find out who is smoking it," said Tawa.

"No," said Glispa. But her sister walked toward the smoke.

She found a campfire where two young men sat. They were out of a dream: tall and straight-backed, with well-trimmed hair and smooth skin. Both wore necklaces of white beads, and one had a mountain lion quiver filled with eagle-feathered arrows.

The young men did not notice the girls.

Tawa said, "Not one man today is as good as these!" She moved forward and smiled.

One of the young men smiled back. He offered her his pipe, and she smoked the sweet tobacco. Glispa hesitated, then joined her.

The smoke whirled around them and danced in sparkling colors. The girls stared at the whirling smoke. Their eyes smarted, but they could not stop watching the dancing patterns. Then, slowly, their eyes slipped down, and both girls slept.

Dawn painted the desert sky the color of a cactus blossom as the girls awoke. The fire was gone, burned to a pile of black ash between them. And other things were not as they had been. Beside Tawa, a bear was stretched. A huge snake coiled itself near Glispa. For these were the real forms of the old men from the battle, who had appeared as young men in the night.

At that very moment, the girls' absence was discovered. In the distance, a shout went up. The warriors were coming for them!

Around them stretched dry land, with mountains rising from the flat plain and deep river ravines. For only a moment Glispa and Tawa hesitated. Beside them were two strange creatures. Behind them were warriors, coming to take them back.

"Come," said Glispa. "I will not go with them," she said, pointing to the magical beings, "and I will not go with them," she said, pointing to the sound of warriors. "Let us find somewhere safe."

The girls began to run. Big Snake and Bear turned themselves again into ancient men and hurried along behind the girls. Behind them, warriors ran in hot pursuit.

The girls ran up Black-Belted Mountain and over Gray Mountain. They ran and ran. They ran for a whole day. They were growing weary, but it seemed they were outrunning the pursuing warriors.

Then, suddenly, the mountain path before them began to move. It writhed and turned and twisted.

The path was covered with snakes. There were black snakes and white snakes, blue snakes and yellow snakes, and silver flashing snakes. They writhed and hissed at the girls.

Tawa stood still as a rock. But Glispa ran right through the writhing mass of snakes. "Come!" she called to Tawa. And her sister ran forward through the hissing path too.

And so the girls continued to run.

At the Rio Grande, the girls ran into the water to hide their footprints. There they agreed it was best to run on separately. Perhaps, this way, one of them would survive. Thus it was that, in the waters of the big river, Glispa and Tawa said goodbye. Weeping, they separated. One ran down the stream, the other ran upstream.

Some say that, after all their adventures, the girls met again as grown women. But most say that there, in the cold river waters, was the last time Glispa ever saw her sister.

Glispa ran up Hosta Butte, over broken rock and thick grass. She ran across Yucca Mountain and over Apache Range. She ran across Black Rock Circle and the Sand Heap. She ran and ran.

Deep in the mountains, she stopped to drink near a herd of wild deer. There she heard a soft sound, like whispering. She looked up and saw a young man standing near her. He wore a rain plume in his hair. His face was painted with blue clay and around his neck hung so many necklaces she could not count them.

"Are you drinking here?" he asked.

"Yes," she said. "I am thirsty. Big Snake is chasing me."

"This is the place of entrance," he said. "Snakes do not know this place." She did not know that he lied. She did not know that he was one of the snake people, luring her to their land.

He took out a weasel-skin pouch and, as he tapped it against a stone, a ladder appeared. Wind rushed from it, singing songs in wind language.

Glispa, alone, climbed down that ladder into the earth.

Inside the earth, she found houses and cornfields. She found fields of melons, but when she tried to pick one it rolled away. Not knowing what else to do, she began walking. Glispa walked until she found a house. Inside were silent people who ate hungrily. They gave Glispa cornmeal, and she too ate hungrily.

Then the people went outside to practice shooting. Some had arrows made of lightning, some had arrows made of rainbows, some had arrows made of snake's bones. Glispa watched the target practice as night gathered like smoke around them.

Then the people came to Glispa. "Stay with us," they said, "stay with us and sleep."

"Yes," said Glispa, her eyes growing heavy.

"But we must tell you something," one of the people said.

"Yes," said Glispa, her head nodding.

"We are snakes," someone said.

The shadowy forms looked like people. She saw no snakes.

"We are snakes," the voice repeated. "Here, in our own land, we look like you while we eat and play and work. But in surface land, we slither and creep. We are what you call snakes."

She had eaten with them, she had watched them play, so Glispa no longer felt fear. She allowed herself to be led into a house, where she fell asleep. Around her, people slept, breathing softly.

When she awoke, it was still night. Glispa had been running for so long that her bones ached. Her knees were swollen, and the bottoms of her feet were bleeding. Suddenly she was frightened, alone in a strange land. She began to rise, to look for help.

The fire was nearly out, so she stumbled. Beneath her feet she saw a coiled snake. Looking around the room she saw them: everywhere, coil upon coil, hundreds of sleeping snakes. They hissed in the night, and their rattles shook a soft song.

She was under the earth with snakes, and there was no escape. Glispa sank back down and lay there—fearful, sad, hurting.

The next morning all the snakes were gone, and Glispa was alone in the house. Suddenly, the old man, Big Snake, entered the house. He was dusty from travelling, and he carried a torch. The girl froze in fear. But he no longer seemed interested in Glispa. He walked right past her and into the inner room. And that was the last she saw of that old man.

Alone in the house, Glispa decided to make a meal. She boiled some water and added a handful of dried corn, just as she did at home. But when she looked over, the corn was boiling out of the pot. She filled a second pot with corn, then a third, then a fourth. She spent the entire day capturing the cooked corn in bowls. When the snakes returned, they mocked her. "Did you not know to add just one kernel to the pot?" they joked. For corn in their world was magical.

The next day they warned her not to touch the water jars. Glispa thought it a silly warning. What would be in the jugs but water? She did not know that one jug contained the rain, another the hail, another the wind. When she grew thirsty, she tipped one over to drink from it. It was the jug of rain, and on earth, people were terrified at the fierce storm Glispa had set loose. The snakes were angry at Glispa when they returned home. But Glispa did not listen to their anger.

Whatever the snakes told her not to do, Glispa did. The next day, she turned over the pot containing the lightning. The day after that, she overturned a pot that caused a dense mist to cover the earth. The snakes objected over and over, but Glispa paid them no heed.

A day came when they told her not to go to the south side of the
house. But of course she did. There she found a dark pool with yel-
low-flowered water plants. Around the water plants jumped hundreds of tiny toads. When they saw her, they all disappeared
beneath the water.

They had gone to fetch their father, Toad Old Man. He rose to
the surface to see who had disturbed his children. When he saw
Glispa, he attacked her in defense of his children. Toad Old Man
was a magician, and the mudballs he threw at her were covered
with curses.

The first one struck her in the leg, the next in the back, the next
in the head. Glispa fell down, unable to move. When the snakes
returned, they thought she was dead. Despite the difficulties she
had caused, the snake-people still cared for the girl. So they called
for Toad Old Man to come back up to the surface of the pool.
They begged him to remove his magic. Sullenly he agreed, and
Glispa rose up again.

But she did not learn. She went to the other side of the house,
even though she was told to stay away. This time she saw rock wrens
playing a game with rocks. It was called rolling-with-stones. The
birds wrapped themselves around rocks and rolled down the hill.

It looked like so much fun! So Glispa tried, too.

But she was no magical bird, and the rock rolled right over her
and did not move. It crushed her completely.

For four days the snakes searched for her. For four days they
could not find her. When they came to the rock wrens, the birds
lied and said no surface-land person had been seen. Four times the
snakes went to the wrens, and four times the wrens lied. But at last
the snakes found out the truth.

It was too late. By the time they lifted the rock from Glispa, she
had been dead so long only bones were left. The snake people sadly
picked up the bones and carried them into the house.

They laid out the bones to create the outline of Glispa's body. She lay there, a skeleton. Then the snake people began to do their most impressive magic: they sang over the white remains of Glispa's body. They sang the most magical of chants, the one called Beauty-way.

At the sound of the snake healing song, magic began to happen. Flesh began to grow again on Glispa's bones. And so the snakes sang harder. Wind began to enter the house. And so they sang harder.

And as the wind blew into Glispa's mouth, they stopped singing and watched as the reborn girl began to breathe.

She woke slowly and looked around. Though she had been dead, she remembered what had happened. She knew she had been sung back to life. From that moment Glispa was changed. She lived each day just to learn what had brought her back to life.

Beauty is what brought her back, and Beautyway is the song and the ceremony.

It took her four years to learn the healing ceremony. Glispa learned the songs. She learned at what point the prayersticks should be used, and the incense burnt, and the sands painted in sacred designs. She learned everything perfectly and did not forget even the smallest action or word. Finally, Glispa was ready to become a healer.

A nine-night sing was held over her. Bright fires were lit. Nettle plants and bearberries were brought out in baskets and fed to the girl. Feathers from bluebirds were brought to her, and magical clothes, and soil from Mother Earth. The snakes sang to Glispa. Four songs they sang, songs that unraveled her inside and remade her, just as her body had been taken apart and remade. In the Dark Circle of Branches the final healing took place. Glispa was complete, changed inwardly, changed outwardly.

As she rose from the final healing, she met a man whom she recognized. He had been singing over her for many days. Looking carefully, she saw the young man from the fire, Big Snake who had grown old and chased her into his country. He was beautiful, more beautiful than any human man she had ever seen. Her heart yearned for him.

But she knew she could not stay with him. Instead, she retraced her steps. Glispa, newborn as a healer, walked out of the lake of snakes and into the surface world. She had won a treasure, and she brought it back proudly. She went back to her village and taught them the songs and the rituals, so that they could be healed by the spirit of beauty.

The girl who had almost been a prize of war brought to her people the greatest prize of all: Beautyway, which brings people into wholeness and health and joy. And even today, whenever the Navaho sing Beautyway, the spirit of the girl Glispa joins them in song.

• • •

## Goddesses of Desert North America

There are 500 nations in North America, nations of people who lived on this continent for countless generations before strangers in sailing ships arrived on their shores. Although the name "Indian" is a misnomer, given to indigenous people by Europeans who thought they had arrived a half a world away on the Indian subcontinent, many Native Americans embrace the term as a general name. But it was not "Indians" or even "Native Americans" whom the Spaniards and the Pilgrims encountered. It was Taino people, and Lene Lenippe, and Penobscott, and Mic-Mac—and hundreds of others. "Indian" is a term like "European," one that does not distinguish among the many different cultures of this continent.

Among these myriad of nations are those of the painted desert of the Southwest: the Hopi, the Apache, the Yaqui, and others. A vast and important nation there is the Navaho, whose distant ancestors had migrated from Asia, across Alaska, and finally down through the central valleys of the North American continent. When they arrived in the beautiful, warm region that is now New Mexico and Arizona, they discovered a fertile homeland where they grew to be a strong and prosperous people.

Women were important in Navaholand, for it was recognized that the mother is the source of all life. In the myths and religious ceremonies of the Navaho, woman's power was honored. Two of the most important divine female figures of the Navaho were Atse Estsan, the first woman, and Estsanatlehi, the turquoise sky-goddess. But it was not only the power of the mother that was revered. Young women's power was regarded as especially significant, as Glispa's story shows.

# Ritual and Magic

Many people think of ritual as something difficult and complicated, something that requires training and occult knowledge. But this is not always true. Every spiritual tradition has rituals, some of which are indeed difficult or complicated. The greatest rituals, like the Navaho Beautyway, are connected with religious understanding, great heroines or divinities, and beautiful artistry. Such rituals are the high point of the ceremonial year or are used to mark the passages of life. In our culture, such rituals as weddings, funerals, and Christmas and Easter ceremonies have similar significance.

But even in ordinary daily life we act out rituals, simple actions we hope will affect our happiness and well-being. Ritual is any action taken with an intention in mind. We dress in a specific way, we fix our hair in a certain way, we wear certain jewelry—all of these are rituals to show people who we are and attract like-minded friends and lovers. We always wear a ring on a certain finger, we always go to school by a certain route, we always have our lunch at a certain table. If we examine these behaviors, we usually find that they are not scientific (the food is not better at the table we choose) but magical (we hope that, if we sit at that table, life will go well that day).

Such ritualized behavior can be completely ineffective. How many times have you punched the call button of an elevator more than once? The mechanism registers the call the first time; further calls do not hurry the elevator along. Yet watch your actions when you are anxious: you push the button once, then again, then again, as though you are speaking in a stern voice to that sluggish machine!

But other ritual actions do have an effect. They change our mental attitude toward the world so that we notice different things and react to things differently. If we think of ourselves as ugly and unattractive, we let our shoulders slouch, fail to keep our clothing looking good, keep our eyes averted. People begin to ignore our inner beauty. But if we smile at our image in a mirror each day and say, "You are beautiful," our shoulders straighten, our eyes sparkle. When people respond to this more approachable person, is it magic? Did the ritual work? No question about it. But it was not the observers who were changed—it was the speaker gazing into the mirror.

The words "ritual" and "magic" are connected. Both describe activities taken to create a change in the external world, in keeping with our inner desires. But the word "magic" has come to be connected with rituals whose source is in ancient religions, such as European earth religions (sometimes called Wicca today) and indigenous American religions. Yet the ritual of lighting candles on Christmas Eve by Christian believers, to celebrate and sustain the inner light of holiness within each of us that corresponds to the Christ child in the manger, is as magical a ritual as any Wiccan ceremony.

Ritual need not be a repeated action; it can be performed once and never again. Ritual need not be a long sequence of actions; it can be a few simple gestures. Ritual does not need to have a specific setting or time; it can be performed anywhere, anytime. Ritual does not need to be something created by someone else, in the dim past; it can be something you create, for yourself, today. Ritual is any kind of action that we undertake to create a change in our outer lives. You already do ritual. As a follower of the young goddess path, you are ready to do it consciously and consistently.

## Creating a Magical Ritual

To create a ritual of your own, you only need two things: a purpose and an action.

The purpose can be general or specific. General rituals are those whose intention is alignment with the world's energies; specific ones have much more narrow targets. For instance, you might choose to celebrate the coming of spring. Such seasonal rituals are found everywhere in the world and serve to join the person or group to the Earth that sustains us. You may also wish to celebrate the phases of the moon as it passes from new to full and back to new again. Suggestions for general rituals are found in this chapter.

In addition to these rituals, people around the world have traditionally celebrated what are called "rites of passage." These are points that mark a person's progress through life. Birth, first menstruation, the selection of a mate, passage into one's crone years, death: these have been the age-old passages of a woman's life. Today we fail to celebrate most of them. But by failing to ritualize the passages of our lives, we also fail to use the power embodied within them. Further suggestions for how to celebrate such rituals are found in chapter 8.

Specific rituals differ from general ones in having a clear, individual purpose. Individuals make their own rituals for innumerable reasons: to get out of debt, to pass an exam, to find a new love, to heal from hurt. Your own reason for creating a ritual might seem inconsequential to someone else, but if your desire for a good grade in math is the most important thing in your life, it deserves a ritual to focus your intention.

To create a ritual of your own, you need to consider what actions are appropriate to the intention you wish to express. Think of it as a pantomime. If you want to show, without words, that you are hungry, what do you do? Make silent gestures of moving food to your mouth? Rub your stomach in an exaggerated circle? Reach out for any passing morsel? All of these gestures would let someone else know that you want food.

You do not have to think of a ritual as showing "someone" what you want—you do not have to imagine offering the ritual to the goddess, to a god, or even to the universe at large. You can, if you wish, address the ritual to yourself, conveying your desires to your unconscious mind. It has been said that dreams are the messengers of the unconscious to the conscious mind, and rituals are the messengers of consciousness to the unconscious. When you perform a ritual, you seed your unconscious mind with intention. In the dark, fertile soil of your dreaming mind, this intention can grow and, later, burst into the light and present you with flowers.

## Rituals for Many Seasons

There are two calendars that have been traditionally used for designing rituals that attune us to the Earth: the solar calendar and the lunar calendar.

### The Solar Calendar

As the Earth passes through its oval orbit around the sun, four points have been noticed by people from ancient times to now. These are:

> **Spring (Vernal) Equinox:** Days and nights are exactly the same length and the season is passing into spring; usually March 21 (dates may vary slightly from year to year). Easter occurs around this time, as does Passover, for this is a turning point that many religions mark. Rituals that show intention of what you want to grow during the next season are appropriate.

**Summer Solstice:** The longest day (shortest night) of the year, when sunlight is at its peak; June 21. Called St. John's Day in some European countries; also called Litha. Rituals of celebration and thanksgiving are appropriate.

**Autumnal Equinox:** Like the spring equinox, but marking the beginning of fall; approximately September 21. Sometimes called Mabon. Rituals of thanksgiving, and of hope for the future, are appropriate.

**Winter Solstice:** The longest night (shortest day) of the year, when sunlight is at its lowest point; December 21. The Christmas holiday occupies the season previously used to celebrate this important solar event. Typical rituals at this time of year celebrate the rebirth of the light in a dark time.

In addition to these dates, there are four other solar feasts that are often celebrated by those practicing earth religions today. These are the cross-quarter days, the old Celtic or Irish holidays.

**Imbolc:** Also called Olmec or Spring's Awakening, the point from which spring arises; February 1. Traditional for initiations and seeding of intentions.

**Beltane:** Sometimes spelled Bealtinne, also called May Day or Lady Day, this is the beginning of the fertile season; May 1. Traditionally marked with the Maypole dance, a festival of fertility and love.

**Lammas:** Also called Lughnasa, a harvest feast celebrated with races and fairs; August 1. Traditional day for betrothals, marriages, and other contracts.

**Samhain:** Pronounced *sow-win* and also called Hallowmas, the day when the veils between this world and the next are lifted, so that the beloved dead can return; the night before is still celebrated as Halloween; November 1. Traditional time for acknowledging the ancestors.

### The Lunar Calendar

The moon's monthly cycle of twenty-eight days was noticed by our ancestors for its connection to the typical woman's menstrual cycle. The phases of the moon are defined in various ways by different cultures, but two of the most common for ritual celebration are the new and full moons.

**New Moon:** When the moon is shadowed by the Earth and its light is not visible, it is said to be a "new moon" and is seen as a seed of possibility. It is an appropriate time for rituals to bring change.

**Full Moon:** When the moon is round and full, even animals are excitable and full of energy. A time for celebration and joy.

## Activities for Magical Wild Girls

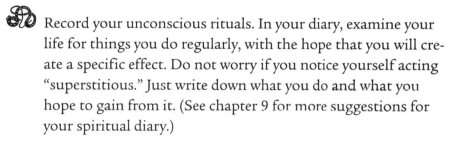 Record your unconscious rituals. In your diary, examine your life for things you do regularly, with the hope that you will create a specific effect. Do not worry if you notice yourself acting "superstitious." Just write down what you do and what you hope to gain from it. (See chapter 9 for more suggestions for your spiritual diary.)

Make a sacred calendar. Get an unmarked calendar, then look up the phases of the moon; draw symbols of the moon on the appropriate dates on the calendar. Make them large enough to see quickly; you may wish to use different colors for the different phases. Next mark the solar holidays on the calendar. Invent appropriate symbols for the seasonal turnings. You may also wish to purchase a calendar with these dates already marked; if you do, make it your own with colored markings, stamps, stickers, or other decorations for each holiday you wish to celebrate.

🪢 Host a seasonal ritual. Select one of the traditional festivals from the list above. Do some research on traditional ways to celebrate the season (see the further reading section for suggestions). Invite some of your friends to create an appropriate ritual with you. You will need several meetings to plan the ritual, as well as the time to do the ritual itself.

🪢 Collect seasonal altar emblems. Look for one small object for each of the four quarters, plus one for each of the four cross-quarters. You can look in natural settings, in thrift stores, through your own closets; you do not need to buy new ornaments. You may choose a little pumpkin for Samhain and a star ornament for winter solstice, for instance. Get a nice box to keep them together on your altar, and at each festival take out the appropriate emblem.

🪢 Collect seasonal costumes. If you wish seriously to celebrate the seasons, you may want to collect costumes appropriate to these events. A black cape for Samhain, a flower crown for Beltane—let your imagination go. Make them yourself out of recycled materials, if possible, to spare the Earth from further depletion of resources.

. . .

# 4

# *Dreamteller in the Land of Death*

## Sumeria

The desert was hot and windy and dry. The earth beneath Gestinanna's feet baked into ruddy clay. The relentless sun shone overhead. The small shrubs and grasses shimmered in the heat.

It seemed a stern land to some, but to Gestinanna it was home, providing her food and shelter and clothing. After her parents' death in the great sickness, Gestinanna had tended their flocks of sheep. She rose each morning to herd them to the green hills, where it was cooler than in the valleys. As they grazed and wandered, she played her flute, or practiced calculation using small pebbles as counters, or made signs in the soil to practice the alphabet the priestesses had invented.

Gestinanna lived alone. Her brother Dumuzi came to visit, staying for a week, sometimes longer. He too was a shepherd, tending sheep from whose wool Gestinanna spun and wove flowing garments. When Dumuzi came in the spring, they killed a lamb in thanksgiving for safe births in their herds. Then they made a feast. Mixed with sour goat's milk or yogurt, the lamb's meat was tasty and fat. They ate companionably together, sitting outside Gestinanna's patchwork leather tent and watching night gather.

In the desert, night came on quickly, with little twilight. In the sudden darkness, the flames of their campfire lit the dark faces of Gestinanna and her brother. Sometimes the girl made music as stars danced in the black sky. Sometimes Dumuzi told stories he had heard on his journeys. He recited the tale of how the hero Gilgamesh found, then lost, the secret of endless life. He told how the dancing girl from the temple tamed the wild man of the hills. He told of how the goddess Inanna stole the treasures from her father Enki as he slept off his drunkenness.

Gestinanna loved hearing these stories. As Dumuzi talked, she watched the moon rise and listened to the desert wind rustling in the scrubby trees. Evening was cool and moist, a relief from the hot, dry day. When they finally could not keep awake a moment longer, they wrapped up in sheepskin blankets and slept by the campfire.

Next morning, they drank fresh milk for breakfast. Sometimes they had tea made from plants that Gestinanna had gathered and dried, or cheese she made from goat's milk—dark brown, heavy cheese, sweet and rich. As they ate, the brother and sister told each other their dreams. Sometimes at night, they knew, gods and demons come into the world. While our body's eyes are open, we cannot see these spirits. But when we sleep, our inner eye can see their magic. Some dreams mean nothing. Too much to eat at dinner, or a daytime worry in disguise. But who can know?

In each family, there is one person who masters the language of dreams. One person who listens in the still morning to the telling of dreams and understands what each dream means. Gestinanna was such a one.

Once Dumuzi dreamed that all the lambs born that spring had died and were being burned in a big fire. The dream frightened him. Did it mean bad fortune? He asked his sister. She laughed, her black hair dancing in its many braids around her brown face. "You are working too hard. The part of you that is just a child—a lamb—wants to play. It feels dead. Your dream bears a message to you: you must not work so hard," she told her brother.

Another time, Dumuzi dreamed a simple dream: of a hot wind blowing through the desert. His heart was pounding when he awoke. It was a silly dream, he told his sister, just a wind on the desert, but—

"That wind," Gestinanna reassured him, "is the breath of life. Sometimes in dreams we come near the source of life. We feel it, we recognize it. But because it is so powerful, it scares us." She reached over the sand and touched her brother's sunburned hand. "You should feel lucky. You have been close to the mystery."

Dumuzi often took his flocks away, across the desert hills, looking for new pasture or visiting old friends. Sometimes a month or more passed before Gestinanna saw his robed figure at the top of a nearby hill. He always waved merrily at her. She flung down her work, leaped to her feet, and waved back. Shortly, she knew, she would hear the jingling of the leader's bells and the tinkle of her brother's camel harness as they sauntered across the sands to her tent.

Gestinanna, too, traveled in search of better pasture. It took time to pack up her belongings onto her camel's back, time to find the sheep who had roamed far on the hillside, time to herd the beasts to another pasture. But as she rode through the hot air, high on her camel, feeling the desert's freedom around her, Gestinanna thought that hers was the best life in the world.

Once the travels of brother and sister took them in different directions for several months. Then, as Gestinanna moved her caravan westward, she came upon a camp. Looking down from the hilltops, she recognized the striped tent of her brother. She gave a loud whoop and slapped her camel's thigh, urging it to run.

When she got to the camp, it was quiet. Quieter than it should be. The tent flap danced in the wind. Dumuzi did not rush out to greet Gestinanna. "He must be gathering wood on the mountain," she thought, brushing aside her concern.

She lifted the tent flap. To her surprise, she saw Dumuzi on his bed. For a panicked moment she thought him ill, but then she saw his head thrashing from side to side and heard him crying, "No! Leave me alone!"

A nightmare. But what was her brother doing sleeping at this time of day? She sat down on the leather bed next to him. "Brother!" she called. "Wake up!" Dumuzi turned, muttering in his sleep. Gestinanna took hold of his left arm and shook it, hard. "Wake up!" she said loudly.

Dumuzi shot up. Staring around, he blinked awake and slowly recognized his sister. "Oh, Gestinanna," he cried. "I had the worst nightmare. There were these—things. They were chasing me. We ran across the desert and over the hills. A couple of times I got snared in brushy trees. The things were horrible—demons, or something. They were red. Horrible!"

The boy shuddered as he talked. Gestinanna sat silent. She, who knew dreams so well, recognized something dreadful about this one.

"Have you ever had a dream like this before?" she asked sternly.

"I've been having them every night. Every night. I can't get any sleep. That's why I was lying down in the middle of the afternoon."

"How long has this been going on?" Gestinanna demanded.

"For a week."

A week. Gestinanna knew that it took exactly a week for demons to reach the earth from the underworld realm. The red ones were servants to Queen Erishkigal, the naked goddess of death. Everyone entered her world when they passed from this life. But sometimes Erishkigal did not wait for you to die. Sometimes she sent her demons to drag you away. And that, Gestinanna knew, was happening to her beloved brother.

A week. That meant the demons were right over the hill, ready to spring on them. Once they had their hands on Dumuzi, there was no escape.

Gestinanna stood up. "Get outside," she ordered. "Get on your hands and knees. Go into my flock of sheep. Not your own—they will look there. Go into mine. Try to make the flock move away from here, but slowly."

She looked around the tent. Her eyes caught the gleam of copper pots and silver ornaments. Where was it?

Then she saw what she wanted. She ran to the corner of the tent and grabbed the skin of a gazelle. She threw it over her brother's head. "Keep this tight around you. And hurry—they're almost here!"

Dumuzi knew his sister was right. She was always right about dreams. He ran outside and plunged into the flock of sheep.

Gestinanna sat down at the flap of her brother's tent and pulled her embroidery from her sleeve pocket. She was calmly threading a needle when the first demon popped his head over the nearby hill.

He was ugly. No doubt about it. Short and round with many arms, with a knobby head and protruding eyes. He was a nightmare come to life. But Gestinanna sat unafraid, concentrating on her sewing.

In a swarm, the demons descended upon her. They surrounded the young woman as she sat on her heels. Calmly, she looked up.

"Who are you?" she asked. "Or maybe I should say, *what* are you?"

"Where is he? Where is he?" shrieked the demons. They jumped up and down wildly. They grabbed Gestinanna's clothing, trying to frighten her. But she knew all about demons. Ugly they might be, but she knew they could not harm her unless commanded by the Queen of Death. She had never seen them in her dreams. So she was safe.

Her brother, however, was in desperate danger. She had to keep the demons' attention away from the sheep flock.

"What do you want?" she asked coldly. "And please answer my other question: what are you?"'

The demons did not stop to answer any questions. They flung the tent flap open and ran inside. They hoisted their puffy little bodies over piles of skins and trade goods that sat in the corners. They peeked with their bulging eyes into leather boxes. They brought a nasty smell into the tent.

Gestinanna stood at the door. "If you want my brother, he isn't here. I don't know where he is right now. I was just waiting for him to return." She got an idea. "Usually he's in the mountains around this time, gathering wood for his cook fire. You might look there."

The leader of the demons shot her a look. The girl kept her face smooth and unruffled, even though she knew it was hard for her to lie without showing it.

The demons ran out of the tent. "Over there," Gestinanna pointed to a distant hill. "That's where he usually goes for wood."

The demons started off in a pack. Then, just as they reached the edge of the camp, they veered to the left and ran directly into Dumuzi's flock of sheep. They yanked the skins off the living animals, killing them instantly.

There was blood everywhere. Gestinanna knew they had a clue as to her brother's whereabouts. But what could she do?

They destroyed the whole flock of sheep, then stood staring at each other and at the hills. They all set off in a pack again. Again, Gestinanna drew a sigh of relief.

Too soon! The demons abruptly turned and ran right past Gestinanna to her sheep. They began tearing off sheepskins. One of the skins came off too easily. And there he was: Dumuzi, her beloved brother, standing in the middle of the dying flock, surrounded by howling demons.

Then the demons and Dumuzi vanished.

Gestinanna stood alone in the blazing sun, bodies of sheep all around her. Vultures drifted in to pick at the carcasses. The sun moved slowly across the sky. She stood like a statue at the entrance to her brother's tent.

Evening came and still she stood. Then, shaking herself as though waking from a dream, she pulled back her hair and tied it behind her ears. She hiked her skirts up above her knees. She grabbed a warm cape from her brother's tent. And she started walking.

She did not know the way to Erishkigal's land, but she would find it. Others had found their way there. She started walking in the dark of the moon, in the desert darkness, in the cold.

She brought no food. She walked straight into the desert, where blowing sand stung her eyes. There was nothing to guide her. She walked over dunes and dunes and dunes. Each of them looked just like the others.

She had brought no water. After a day she was exhausted and thirsty. Passing a couple of desert plants, she broke them open and drank their juices. But soon she was beyond even that. She walked on, on, on, her feet growing heavier, her eyes growing dimmer.

Then she fell. She could not move. Sand began to blow over her, to bury her. She could see her legs being buried, then her arms. But she was so weak that she could not move them or brush the sand away. Her eyes grew dimmer and dimmer.

Gestinanna died on the desert dunes.

She did not know it, but she had done just the right thing. As she died, she found herself at the entrance to Erishkigal's kingdom.

She passed the gatekeeper, a fierce skeleton. She found herself on a long, dark, endless plain. Dimly, in the distance, she saw a light. As she walked closer, it took shape.

It was a woman, huge and glowing. It was Erishkigal.

The goddess lay asleep. Long, black hair flowed behind her giant head. All around her were thousands of ghosts. Some clung to her chest, some nestled around her knees, some were tangled in her hair. They, too, were asleep.

It was not a bad place, Erishkigal's world. Everyone slept, everyone had dreams. But it was not the world above. It was not a land of sunshine and night, of hot wind and bitter chill, of winter and summer. It was a dim, dull world in which no one ever wakened, played, sang, or loved. Gestinanna hated to think of her brother there forever.

She saw him as she approached. He was the only one in the scene she could really see. Other spirits there were a soft, empty color, their clothes transparent. But Dumuzi had been stolen, still living, from the earth, so his skin was still a rich brown, and he still wore bright, woven desert garments.

Gestinanna approached. She walked up to the giant Queen of Death. "Erishkigal," she called.

The queen shuddered in her sleep. She did not like to awaken. She liked to sleep, eons and eons at a time. In her dreams she guided the world: who would die, who would live. She did not waken fully, but opened a single eye dreamily.

She saw a tiny figure, not entirely faded, someone recently dead. The figure was waving her arms and shouting. This was unseemly behavior. The Queen of Death awakened fully.

She did not sit up. She opened her huge eyes and stared at Gestinanna.

Gestinanna shouted, "You have stolen my brother. You must give him back his life. You can have me instead."

And it was true. She was dead, this Gestinanna, but Erishkigal had not sent orders for her. Gestinanna had come of her own accord.

Erishkigal did not remember exactly why she had sent her demons to fetch Dumuzi. Some argument with the goddess Inanna, something she'd already half-forgotten. But now that he was here, the goddess had taken a fancy to Dumuzi. She wanted him to stay. Her sleep would be more comfortable in his presence. Erishkigal did not want to give him up.

Held down by demons, Dumuzi fought to come to Gestinanna's side. He struggled against the ugly, warty creatures. Finally he freed himself from their grasp and ran to his sister.

He clutched her arm. "What are you doing here?" But she was fading into nothingness. Dumuzi's hand slipped through Gestinanna's flesh. He stared at her, not quite believing she was dead.

The Queen of Death watched the pair. She could see how much they cherished each other. A kindly goddess, she took the sick and the old into her arms. She wanted those who would be happier sleeping in her arms than on the earth. And so she spoke.

The gray world of Erishkigal heard her voice, a deep sound like a person talking in sleep. "You cannot go back to the earth together, because one of you is dead, and the dead cannot return."

Dumuzi and Gestinanna looked at each other. "Then we shall both stay!" Dumuzi started to say, but Gestinanna shook her head.

"I am dead. I must stay," she said to Erishkigal. "Release my brother."

"Do not tell a goddess what to do," Erishkigal told her. But the girl's love for her brother touched her. "I will tell you my decision. Dumuzi may go. But in six months, he must return. Then you shall go to take his place on the earth. At the end of your life span, I will have you both."

"When my life is over, we will be together," Dumuzi called out to his sister. He was already fading, disappearing from the land of death. Gestinanna had won life for her brother. Only half a life, but enough. She felt a pang of longing. She would never sing to Dumuzi again. Never hear his stories, brought from the towns to her desert camp. Never tell him the meaning of his dreams.

But she did not have time to grieve. Gestinanna was already sinking into sleep. Dreams would come there, dreams such as she had never known. She drifted into the arms of Erishkigal, her goddess.

Dreams overcame her, and Gestinanna slept.

• • •

## Goddesses of Sumeria

More than three thousand years ago, a civilization arose on the plains of the eastern Mediterranean, in what is now called Iraq. Between two great rivers, the Tigris and the Euphrates, the ancient land called Sumer stretched with its cities and farms. The culture, called Sumerian, was that of several important centers of the ancient world. Babylon, Assyria, Chaldea—these were the names of some of the Sumerian kingdoms in the cradle of civilization. There, laws were written down for the first time. There, mathematics and writing and astronomy were invented.

Sumeria was a place where women played vital roles in all aspects of life. Inside the cities' high stone walls were pyramidal temples, called ziggurats. Many were dedicated to goddesses, invoked as the highest powers of the land. Inside, priestesses conducted ceremonies. They were scholars; writing was probably invented by priestesses to keep temple records. In its mythology and religion, the Sumerians gave an important place to women.

One of the greatest Sumerian myths concerns the great goddess Inanna's descent into the realm of death, of which the story of Gestinanna is a portion. In the songs and invocations that tell Inanna's story, we find that of Gestinanna and her devotion to her brother—a story more than 3,000 years old, but still new today.

## Recalling and Interpreting Dreams

Almost every civilization has recognized the importance of dreams. In ancient times there were dreaming hospitals, where sick people would spend the night sleeping. The next day, dream doctors would speak with them about the dreams and what secrets they held. These dream doctors believed that mind and body were not separate, and that when the body was ill, the reasons—and the cures—could be found in the dreaming mind.

Many civilizations, too, believed that we enter a real world when we dream. In Australia, the world of spirit is called "the Dreamtime." The indigenous people of that continent believe that, in dreams, we come close to another reality, one filled with gods and goddesses, one where there is no time nor space to hinder us. In Sumeria, too, dreams were believed to be powerful ways to discover the spiritual realities of our lives.

Today, however, we dismiss the powerful images of our sleeping minds with the words, "Oh, it's just a dream," as though dreams are false, unreal, even silly. But the power and truth of dreams has not changed. It is only we who have stopped recognizing how to use them.

You can begin to put the power of dreams into action in your life by remembering and recording them. You can then begin to interpret them. You may wish to do this by yourself or with a group of trusted friends. Do not tell your dreams to just anyone. They are the secrets of your soul. Why trust them to strangers?

To begin this process, you need to remember your dreams. Probably you were told, as a child, that dreams did not matter. Or, if you reported a frightening dream, you were consoled by someone telling you that it was not real. As a result, many of us lose access to our dreams. We still dream, but our disbelief has caused the dreams to retreat to a place beyond our memories. It may take a bit of time for the dreams to surface again, if you have discouraged yourself from being aware of them.

Even if you have continued to be aware of dreaming, catching actual dreams before they escape takes some practice. How often will you lie there, thinking you cannot possibly forget that vivid dream about the man with his hair on fire, only to find you have no clue *what* you were dreaming about once you finally get up?

To capture dreams, you will need to set up a system for recording them. Placing a notebook and writing implement by the bedside is a good way to begin. As you first close your eyes at night, hold in your mind the intention of remembering whatever dreams come to you. Set your alarm to mild music rather than a loud buzz. Lie abed for a moment before you rise, collecting your dreams. Then write them them down immediately. Even waiting until after breakfast allows dreams to escape. Date the dreams before or after recording them, so you can later look to see what connection the dreams have to waking life.

After you have recorded dreams for a few months, you can start interpreting them. A good interpretive rule is this: everything and everyone in the dream is you. When you dream about a teacher being cruel to you, that means the teacher-you is giving trouble to the student-you. Examining your life, you may discover negativity about something you are trying to learn. Your mind, recognizing this, holds up a mirror to your action. Naturally, your mind will select, from images and memories it has stored, an appropriate symbol of your inner conflict. The teacher of whom you dream may, in fact, be mean to you. Why else would your dream pick that image for your inner negativity?

In your dreams, you will encounter many images of your inner self: the child, who appears when you are filled with potential; the shadow, your negative self whom you must learn to accept; your inner masculine energy, which all women have (as men have inner feminine energy); and your secret wisdom, which often appears as a wise old woman (or man). All of these figures are you. So is the cat who walks saucily down the street, the frightening wolf in the window—and even the street, and the window, are part of you, too!

## Forming a Dream Group

One way to explore dream interpretation is to work with a group of trusted friends. If you have formed a Wild Girls' group, you may decide on this as one of your regular activities. Or you may have other friends who might wish to participate in such a search. Age does not matter, and neither does location; you could be part of an online dream group. Men and women, boys and girls, all can benefit from dream interpretation.

What is important is that everyone agrees to follow the rules of the group. You will be sharing your secrets—some things so secret that even you do not quite understand them. Should you feel that someone in the group is being disrespectful, stop attending. The other members may decide that the offending person should leave, in which case you can rejoin. Never stay in a group with someone who uses your dreams to make fun of you, to manipulate or coerce you, or to be cruel to you. Your dreams are a healing part of your life, not something you should be ashamed of.

If you follow a very simple process, one used by dream groups around the world, your group will be helpful and cooperative. The four-step process, invented by the psychologist Montague Ullman, is this: one person tells a dream. The others ask questions about any part of the dream they do not understand. Then each person interprets the dream, starting with the words "If this were my dream . . ." Finally, the dreamer discusses what she has learned from the group discussion.

The most important part of this process is the words "If this were my dream . . ." Each speaker imagines that she had the dream. If the dreamer says, "My father walked into the room," each person talks about her father, not the original dreamer's. This keeps the interpretation from turning into amateur diagnosis: "This is a dream about how bad you feel because Jason doesn't like you." If any member of the group fails to follow the rules, any member—including the original dreamer—has the right to ask her to stop.

When the group members have offered their "if this were my dream" interpretations, the original dreamer concludes the discussion by explaining how she interprets the dream. Comments by other group members will often open up new realms of understanding. No comment is useless, but each dreamer has the right to accept as relevant only those that speak to her.

Usually dream groups meet once a month. You do not need to interpret every dream you have. Select ones that puzzle you. Once you've been offered possible interpretations, write in your dream diary about what you believe the dream means. This way, you can go back as you develop your dream interpretation skill and add further ideas and information.

## Making Your Own Dream Dictionary

Every dreamer has an individual vocabulary of images, one that comes from her life experience. Someone who grew up in Alaska will have a different inner landscape than someone who grew up in Florida. So do not bother buying someone else's dream dictionary. Make your own, one filled with your own inner images.

To start, you will need some dreams. Record as many as you can for a few months before starting to compile your dictionary. Then go through and list characters and settings and objects from your dreams. Next to each entry, write a list of words you associate with that person or thing. Do not think about what others would expect you to write. If, when you think of flowers, you think of funerals, write that down. Do not write "pretty, fragrant, happy" just because you think others would expect you to interpret flowers that way. For you, a cat might indicate cruelty (cats kill birds, after all), a restaurant might represent danger (if you once got food poisoning there), and a sandy beach might represent work (if you had a job as a lifeguard).

Some dream images might have more than one meaning. In fact, an image can have two meanings that are entirely opposite of each other. A police officer can represent safety (the part of you that attempts to keep order) and violence (the part of you that strikes out at anything that challenges that order) at the same time. Or you might find characters that turn into other characters, or settings that seem composed of several familiar places. These are your mind's way of showing you a mixture of qualities you have not yet encountered in waking life. As you write down your associations, be sure to include your memories and interpretations of all parts of the image.

## Characters

The characters in your dreams are all parts of you. As you add each person to your dream dictionary, ask yourself what qualities or actions you associate with that person and write that down. As you use your dream dictionary to interpret your dreams, never forget that everything in the dream is you. If you associate a teacher with being strict, you are dreaming about your own inner strictness. If you dream of someone from school whom you think is pushy, that is your own aggressiveness appearing in the dream. Characters can include:

Real-life characters (your mother, a teacher, a friend)

Famous people (rock stars, politicians, celebrities)

Historical figures (from any era or country)

Mythological or fantasy figures (from books, movies, television)

Professional figures (judges, police, nuns)

Groups of figures (a theater troupe, a motorcycle gang)

Unknown figures (be sure to record any details of appearance or clothing)

Composite figures (your dad who seems to be a judge)

## Animals

Animals frequently appear in dreams. They point to our wilder nature, the part of us that is not yet human and civilized. Write down qualities you associate with each animal, and any specific memories.

Pets (whether living or not)

Wild animals (ones you have encountered in zoos or in the wild, ones you have read about or seen on television)

Mythic animals (from books, movies, television)

Composite creatures (dogs that act like bears)

## Settings

Dream settings tell you about the part of your life to which a dream is connected. When you dream of a place you vacationed, ask yourself what memories you have from that place. When you dream of a familiar place altered in some way, record both your ideas about the real place and its changes. Pay attention to whether the dream takes place indoors or outdoors, as this can reveal whether you are dreaming of something in your internal life or your outer one. Also pay attention to your feelings about the place, and whether they seem appropriate or inappropriate; a usually comfortable room that seems threatening in a dream may be your mind's way of drawing attention to an inner difficulty.

Home (both indoor and outdoor)

Vacation places (indoor and outdoor)

Imaginary places (seen on television or movies, read about in books)

Composite places (parts of real and/or imagined places combined)

Altered places (real places with something changed about them)

## Objects

Objects that appear in dreams are parts of you, just as people and settings are. Any object, from a book to a piece of furniture, is important to interpreting a dream's meaning. Objects that appear frequently in your dreams are gifts from the spirit. In many dream traditions, such objects should be created in the waking world. If you dream of a necklace, make that necklace or have it made. Even making a drawing of a dream object can bring you closer to your inner power.

Plants (flowers, trees, vines, houseplants)

Jewelry and clothing

Furniture and paintings

Sculptures and statuary

Food

Machines

## Activities for Dreamy Wild Girls

 When you wake up, or are awakened, in the middle of a dream, write down what you remember. Then ask a friend or friends to join you in acting it out. When you get to the end, let the play continue. How does the dream end when you act it out?

 Make a dream pillow. Use a piece of fabric that has some meaning for you: a piece of an old garment, a part of a friend's tee shirt, something in a significant color. You do not need much; the pillow can be as small as your fist. Cut two squares of equal size. Using hand or machine stitching, sew three sides of the pillow together. Then fill with hops, an herb that traditionally has been used to induce sleep and is available in health-food stores. Finish the pillow by turning under the remaining side and hand-sewing it closed; make the stitches as inconspicuous as possible. You might want to decorate the dream pillow with a symbol or symbols from your dreams.

Make a dreamcatcher. The Ojibway (Chippewa) people of the northern Midwest made these to catch good dreams but keep bad ones away. If you are Ojibway by heritage, find an elder who can assist you in creating a dreamcatcher, and be sure to dangle some feathers from it to make it especially powerful. If you are from a different heritage (see chapter 10 regarding the importance of heritage in spirituality), you can create your own version of a dreamcatcher by finding a supple piece of wood—a thin branch of willow is good. Or use metal if you have no access to wood; coat hangers are hard to shape, but flexible wire is readily available at craft stores. Form it into a circle and tie it together, using ribbons or yarn. Then, using the same ribbons or yarn, create a web inside the circle. Leave portions open for good dreams to pass through. As you create this dreamcatcher, fill it with your intention that you will understand the meaning of your dreams.

 If you have trouble remembering your dreams, try this: every night, just before you go to bed, write down five words. Do not look at the words for at least a month. Just keep writing them down. When a month has passed, look over your lists and see what words appear frequently. What do the words tell you about yourself?

 Do a dream drawing. Use a dream that you found especially difficult to understand. Using any medium (crayons, chalk, paint, or even pencil), draw a significant scene from the dream. Do not do this quickly. Draw one line, then put down your drawing implement. Stare at the drawing until you see where the next line should be. The drawing may be different from the dream in one or more ways. You will be revealing more about what the dream means as you draw.

· · ·

# 5

# *White Shoulders, White Wings*

## Ireland

It was midnight on the longest night of the year. Finola was sound asleep when someone awakened her. "You must come to your father," the servant said, insistently. Finola rose into the chill dampness, rubbing her eyes and pulling her wool cloak tightly around her.

In the big central room of their home, her father sat staring into the smoky fire. Finola wrapped herself tightly in her cloak as she waited for him to speak. Finally he did so. "The queen," Lir began. Then he stopped and sighed. "The queen . . . she is . . . is dying."

Finola shivered. This queen? The second? Was there a curse on their family? Her own mother, Ava, had died after giving birth to little Conn. She had never recovered, sinking instead into an endless sleep in which she breathed her last. But that had not been like this. This strange fever came from nowhere. Not even the healers could find what caused the queen's distress.

Gentle Ava's death had desolated Finola, who had cried for weeks. Other girls' mothers—even mean ones, even greedy ones—lived on. But Ava was dead. It was so unfair! Finola had fallen ill with grief.

At first Finola held Conn responsible for her loss. But how could anyone stay angry at the ruddy infant with the big hazel eyes? It was not long before Finola had dismissed the servants to care for Conn herself. Later she took over the care of Fiachra and Aed too. She loved them as much as any mother would—as much as their own mother had. Lir did what he could to help, but he was a busy king. So it was Finola who washed the boys' skinned knees and bandaged their cuts. It was Finola who taught them the stories of their ancestors. It was Finola who taught them the songs of their land.

Each night, the boys nestled into their blankets as Finola sang them to sleep. After Lir had kissed her goodnight, Finola pulled her cloak tight and walked across the courtyard to the feather-thatched sunhouse where she slept.

Finola was young to bear the burdens of motherhood. But she found them to her liking. She told her father so, when he decided to marry again. "But it is for your sake," Lir told her. "You have had no childhood, bearing these woman's burdens so soon."

Finola shrugged. Childhood seemed all useless pleasures. She saw girls in other families dreaming of their futures while they passed the long, soft days in games and chatter. She did not envy them. Her own days brought new responsibilities, new challenges. How to keep Aed from teasing Conn so much? How to get Fiachra to remember his chores? How many woolen socks do three boys need in winter?

The servants bowed to her when she passed, as though she were a queen already. Even the chiefs who visited her father listened silently when she spoke. No girl of twelve in another province was treated with the respect accorded Finola. "I do not wish to trade my life," she told her father, "to become a child again."

But Lir had made his decision. He had only to find the right woman. Of the ten levels of marriage, this king wanted only the highest. He could marry a poor woman, a foreigner, even a fairy. But he wanted a marriage of equals, as he had with Ava. And there were few woman in Ireland as noble in blood and property as Lir was.

Finally he chose a noblewoman from the next province. Aeife arrived by chariot for the wedding, a tall woman with piercing eyes. Finola felt something odd—something cold around her heart—the moment she looked at the queen. She thought about talking to her father about her feeling. She thought about asking to be sent as a foster child to a relative's house. But she wanted her father to be happy, and she wanted to be near him, so she ignored what she had felt. That mistake caused all the pain to follow.

The wedding dance brought nobles from all four provinces. The celebration went on for days, with feasting and dancing and drinking and singing. When the last guest, a wandering poet, had departed, the household settled down to begin its new life.

Instead, they found life soon became just as it had been before. Once again, a queen lay sick and dying. Aeife twisted and turned in pain. Her forehead was perpetually hot, her eyes rolled feverishly in her head. The dull glass windows were kept closed, covered by their brass shutters.

For Finola, it was as though there had been no marriage. She still cared for the boys and sang them to sleep at night. Sometimes she felt guilty for her happiness, for the new queen seemed to suffer indeed. But Finola was glad to be out of Aeife's sight, for she was afraid.

She was afraid the queen might bewitch her. Her fear had started at the wedding dance, when one of the servants from

Aeife's former home gossiped to a servant of Lir's. Soon everyone in the village was saying it: Aeife was a magician. And an evil magician at that.

The boys joined in with the tale-telling about the queen's supposed magic, though Finola tried to discourage them. They always exaggerated! Besides, they might say something at the wrong time and cause trouble. So she shook her head whenever her little brothers brought her their latest rumors of Aeife's powers. The new queen, they told her, had once turned a servant girl into a stick for not being fast enough with her work. Magicians have different powers. Aeife, it seemed, had the magic of transformation.

Even though Finola believed the tales, she shook her head at the boys' tales. Pursing her lips, she shook her head. "I told you not to believe everything you hear," she said sternly.

"But the servants say—"

"They also say that there's a spell on Lough Darga, that big old lake, and that we shouldn't swim there or we'll turn into frogs," Finola reminded them. They had all swum there on hot summer days, and none had become frogs. The boys said nothing more— that day—about the queen's magic.

Finola always told herself that she was a girl with no magic. She could not read minds or hearts. She could not make things into other things. She could not cast spells. Some were born with power, some were not. Finola told herself that she had only the powers of an ordinary girl.

But even the most ordinary girl has the power to recognize those who want to hurt her. That is magic, because to know your enemies is to read their hearts and minds. But Finola did not believe in her own magic. She did not listen to her heart. When she seen Aeife that first day, she had felt like a sparrow beneath a swooping hawk. But she had put that feeling aside. Finola would learn to trust herself, but first there would be much suffering.

From her sickbed, Queen Aeife called the king to her side. She had an idea, she told him in a hoarse whisper. They must send her to a magician, the most powerful magician in all Ireland. He would make her well.

"Bodb," said Lir. Aeife nodded weakly.

It happened that the most powerful magician in the land was Bodb, Ava's father, Finola's grandfather. A fierce old man, he would turn away a woman of strange blood, especially one who had replaced his own daughter in her household. Lir told Aeife that.

"Send Finola with me," said the queen.

King Lir thought about that. It seemed a good idea. If Aeife arrived with Bodb's own kin, he would certainly take care of her.

And so it was agreed: Finola and her brothers would travel to the far west, to Bodb's land, with the new queen. The very next morning, Finola pulled herself from bed to pack a leather bag of clothes. Then she trudged out to the main house. Lir stood there already with the boys, watching as Aeife, pale and weak under her furs, was carried to a chariot. Lir kissed Finola and hugged the boys. Then they climbed on the chariot and, in a shriek of bronze wheels, they were gone.

For half a day they traveled. They went more slowly then they intended, for the queen often cried out in pain, and they were forced to stop while she recovered. At one of these stops, they found themselves on the edge of Lough Darga.

The queen asked to be taken from the chariot to sit by the water's edge. "I love the look of the blue ponds near my old home," she said in a sad voice.

*Was she dying?* Finola thought in fear. People's minds often wander as they neared death. But the queen seemed stronger. She ordered the soldiers to a nearby farm to purchase fresh milk. The children rambled around the lakeshore, throwing stones into the placid waters.

A mist had fallen that morning, as it did on most mornings in Ireland. But now the soft mist lifted. The sun came out, and the air began to steam in the heat. The soldiers had not yet returned.

"Let us take a swim, Finola!" little Conn begged.

A feeling—fear?—gripped Finola's heart. She started to shake her head. Then she saw Aeife, smiling.

"Let them swim," she said weakly. "It will make me happy." So Finola agreed, though her heart felt like a sparrow under the shadow of a hawk.

The three boys were soon wading happily in the shallow water near the shore. Finola, slipping out of her cloak and overdress, ran out after them. She did not want to let the boys swim alone.

As soon as they were all in the water, Finola saw the queen rise to her feet and lift her right arm. Finola looked over her shoulder to see what Aeife was warning them against.

She was pointing at Aed. She was saying something. Finola could not hear it, but Aed was splashing around furiously.

Finola began to wade toward him when she saw Aeife pointing at Fiachra, who began splashing too. Then the queen pointed at Conn, and this time her voice—which had grown louder and louder—rang across the lake. Aeife was chanting:

*A swan you are:*

*Three hundred years on this lake,*

*Three hundred on the Sea of Moyle,*

*And yet three hundred on Inish Glora.*

She was using the magician's formula! Again the leaden feeling in Finola's heart. And then the queen was pointing at her. This curse was different:

*Three curses on you, girl child:*

*Nine hundred years a swan,*

*Three boys to care for always,*

*A heart heavy with loss, loss, loss.*

Finola felt the curse travel across the water, uncoil, and hit her. A tingle on her arm, then white feathers sprouting. Her neck pulled forward, straightened, lengthened. Her feet stretched out into webbed claws on the sandy lake bottom.

"Boys!" Finola called as the terror of the queen's curse hit her heart like a rock. "Boys!"

Finola saw them near her. But they were no longer splashing, carefree boys. They were swans, three white swans. Finola looked down at her own white body. It was sleek and feathered—for she too was a swan.

On the shore, she saw soldiers returning. The queen, pretending to cry, pointed at the lake. The soldiers helped Aeife into the chariot. The queen and her escorts left.

The three boys swam to their sister, whining in fear. Startled, Finola realized they were speaking in human voices. As she felt emotion swell in her heart, she knew the change was not complete. The queen had left their minds and hearts to suffer, and to know that they were suffering.

That night, Finola built her first nest, a makeshift home of twigs and soggy leaves. The next day, Finola and her brothers awoke to see an ugly, skinny crane fly over them, screaming. Finola shuddered. So this would be their life now, among wild birds and beasts.

And, indeed, such was their life. For the first fifty years, there were a few moments each day to remind Finola of her life as a girl. Lir moved his household to the shores of Lough Darga. Each evening, Finola floated ashore to spend a few hours sitting with her father. They would talk quietly together. Lir told her over and over how Aeife had pretended to be sick in order to destroy the children. How old Bodb tried to lift Aeife's curse, but found it beyond his power. How, in revenge, Bodb had turned Aeife into a bird, a squawking crane. But these stories did not console the girl trapped within a swan's skin.

Years passed. Lir grew gray and stooped. Then one day Finola swam ashore to find her father's bench empty. The next month, the houses of the village fell silent. Lir was dead. Now the empty years would have no relief.

But more than two centuries were left for the children of Lir to swim Lough Darga's waters.

Never in those years did the boys grow up. They were as impetuous and irresponsible as swans as they had been as boys. Finola, knowing she could have saved them all if she had listened to her heart that first day, learned to trust herself. Season after season, Finola watched her brothers, made nests for them at night, and guarded them from hunters.

Year after year, Finola watched people stop by the lake to admire their swanny loveliness. With a sad heart, she remembered times when she, too, had stood watching swans glide past. She, too, had thrown tidbits into the water—as people threw food to her now. Sometimes young girls, their feet dragging in the water, called out to her. Girls her age, the age she had been when Aeife enchanted her. Sometimes a boy and a girl, new to love, walked hand in hand by Lough Darga. They stopped, the girl resting her head on the boy's shoulder as he pointed to the floating swans. Then Finola's heart wept for what she had missed of human life.

Years passed. The girls she had seen those first summers on the lake now walked past with their children. Then those children passed with their first loves, while girls of other years hobbled along on canes. Generations came and went, kingdoms rose and fell, and the children of Lir ceased to remember what year they had been enchanted. They no longer counted how many years were left.

The people of Ireland, too, slowly forgot the old legend of enchanted swans with the voices of humans. Sometimes, in deep winter when ice threatened their watery home, the children crushed their wings together and sang laments for their lost lives. Thus each generation of Irish countryfolk told afresh the tale that swans could sing. The names of the children who were the singers were gone, lost to memory. But the curse still held them enchanted.

Three hundred years passed on Lough Darga. Then Finola and her brothers took wing to the freezing Sea of Moyle. Three hundred years they spent there, on a stormy sea where they were often separated, where sometimes they thought each other dead. Then, finally, the children of Lir had only three hundred years left to spend on Inish Glora, a little lake-studded island in the Atlantic.

There the tale of the singing swans was lost, for there was no one to hear them and keep the story alive. On their empty island, Finola and her brothers no longer saw the way styles of clothing changed, or the design of the tools used to work the fields. Time stood still for them on lonely Inish Glora.

But years, uncounted, still pass. And so one day, at last, nine hundred years had flown since Aeife had stood to cast her curse.

The children of Lir were floating that day in a small lake when they heard distant voices. Finola swam down a little inlet and peered across the water. Boats were skimming from the mainland. Finola gathered her brothers and swam further inland, nestling them in a reedy patch.

The boys were as noisy as ever. Finola tried to quiet them, without effect. But it did not matter, for the boats were filled with berry-picking women, not hunters looking for plump birds to roast.

A girl spied the swans. She called to others, and soon the lakeshore was dotted with admiring women.

From their bags came crumbs of bread. The boys dived for the food, to girlish squeals. Soon Fiachra was eating out of the girls' hands, then the other brothers as well. Finola paddled somberly in the water nearby, watching. In her deepest heart she knew something important was about to happen.

Just then the sun, which had been hidden in a cloudbank, burst forth. At that same moment, the feathers dropped from the enchanted children.

With a gasp, the girls fell back from the water's edge. Finola looked around her happily. They were the same age, wearing the same clothes, as they day when they were cursed. She smiled a little as she realized how strange they must look to these women.

From the crowd on shore, a tall woman stepped forward. "I am Queen Decca," she said solemnly, raising her hand with the royal ring upon it. "Welcome, strangers, to my land."

"And we," Finola began, "are the children of Lir."

But she could not go on. Before her eyes, she saw her brothers aging. This moment they were boys; the next, young men; the very next, old men. Then they were men older than any the world had ever seen.

Finola saw, from the horrified look on the queen's face, that the same transformation was passing over her own body. All their nine hundred years were sweeping through the children of Lir. In moments, they would be dust.

Finola spoke in a whisper. "My brothers, I love you." Her voice was already like fading mist. But she had one more message. To the queen and her women she said, "Believe your heart!" And then she was gone.

In one moment, the children of Lir collapsed in the sand of Inish Glora and disappeared. Before the stricken eyes of the women, dust rose in four little whirlwinds and blew out to sea.

The women stood like statues on the shore. The sun went behind a cloud, leaving the western island in gloom again. Queen Decca looked long out to sea before she spoke.

"Goodbye," she said finally in a sorrowful voice, "goodbye, children of Lir. We who were sent to see you die will find out who you were. And wherever there are people of your blood, your names will be remembered. The love of a sister for her brothers will be sung in songs across this island. And women will never forget your message to listen to our own hearts."

Decca motioned to her women. They turned to leave. As they filed silently back to their boat, the last woman—the youngest—stooped suddenly. When she stood, she held cradled in her hands a single white swan feather.

• • •

## Goddesses of Ireland

Among the myths and legends of ancient Ireland, one of the most famous is that of Finola and her brothers, the children of Lir. Told and retold for more than a thousand years, it has inspired songs, plays, poems, paintings, and sculpture. It is one of the treasures of the Irish people.

Finola's story dates from a time when Ireland honored Celtic divinities served by Druid priests and priestesses. Among these were the great goddess Brigid, whose name comes into our language as Bridget, goddess of fire and the sun, of water and healing. There was Danu, the great mother whose breasts formed the hills of the Irish southwest. There was wild Maeve, the splendid warrior. Magical Edain, whose children became heroes. Liadan the singer. Luaths Lurgann, the fleet runner.

There was the banshee who wailed before someone died. Bo Find, the cow goddess of abundance, with her magical lake in the west. The stern Cailleach, the hag whose features are written on the stony cliffs. The even fiercer Morrigan, who appeared sometimes as a crow, sometimes as a giant. And river goddesses whose names still flow across the land, Sinann (the Shannon) and Boann (the Boyne).

The Irish Celts came in ancient times, migrants to a land where other goddesses had been worshiped for many thousands of years. Although we do not know their names, we can see the faces of these goddesses in huge caverns, where spirals fill the stony walls. Goddesses have been honored in Ireland for as long as 6,000 years. Their stories are told even today in the green spring and the dark winter, by poets and singers, by mothers and sisters and giggling girlfriends. Like Finola, the great tales of Ireland live on, and on, and on.

## The Power of Words

The Celtic people believed fiercely in the power of words. To them, the bard or poet was a magician, someone who could change the world by words alone. The childish saying "Sticks and stones will break my bones, but names will never hurt me" was never spoken by a Druid. There were, in fact, ten kinds of Celtic curses based in the magic of words. One curse was inventing a name for someone—a name so nasty and so appropriate that the person could never shed it.

Names do hurt, despite what the childish slogan says. Like any ritual, the repetition of words affects us. If someone calls you a derogatory name, some part of you will believe that it is true. And the words do not have to be spoken by others. If you constantly repeat to yourself, "I'm a terrible dancer," you will avoid dancing. By not dancing, you will grow stiffer and more clumsy. Your own negative imaginings will finally become real. You may not have started out as a bad dancer, but you will end up that way.

We still have many superstitions that acknowledge how powerful speech is. Nicknames, for instance, are common. You might think we use nicknames because they are shorter or easier to say. But "Susie" has the same number of syllables as "Susan." No savings of breath there! And some nicknames, like Buddy or Sis, are completely different than the actual name. Why do we do this? Because of the Irish belief that fairies, attracted to human babies, will steal them away if they know their real names. Using a false name—a nickname—kept children safe. That we still use nicknames today is a testament to the hidden power of such beliefs.

The Celts were not alone in recognizing the power of words. Most ancient cultures believed that words not only express, but help form, our reality. Rituals often were based on singing or chanting powerful words. Names of divinities were especially effective as prayers for healing.

It is easy to think that the magic lies in the words themselves, that the word "abracadabra" makes the genie appear. But if you do not expect a genie when "abracadabra" is chanted, the magic does not work, because the word itself does not create magic. Like any ritual (see chapter 3), words bear messages to our deep mind, from which change is born.

We do not have to speak magical words aloud. Merely saying them in our minds can bring results. But using the voice amplifies the power of the message. So does the use of rhythmic speech, sensual imagery, and pleasing sounds. Poetry and magic are deeply connected. Using poetry to affect change in our world was one of the secrets of those distant Celts among whom Princess Finola lived.

# Creating a Healing Charm

There are two main forms of verbal magic: the charm and the curse. Both are used to create change. The difference is that the charm brings pleasant changes, while the curse brings negative or even painful ones.

In the story of Finola, her magician-stepmother Aiefe caused the children to turn into swans just by screaming a curse at them. Why did she not just yell, "You! You're a swan!" while waving her arms about? What was the point of the magic formula of three parts? Did it really have more power than simple sentences?

The Celts and other traditional people believed that words have more power when carefully arranged, rather than randomly spoken. Rhymes, which stick in the mind like burrs, were used to create easy-to-remember songs and chants. Once remembered, they could be repeated until the sought-after effect was gained. There are, in addition, many teachings about the secret significance of certain sounds.

But you do not have to be a lifelong magician to use words in magical ways. You can do so by learning various traditional poetic forms, ones based in magic. One such form is the Old English charm. When we say someone is "charming," we mean they have a magical effect, just like this kind of poem. Like most pieces of verbal magic, the charm has strict rules. Beginning with one feature of a person or situation, you turn it into another by saying that it is so. You say, "May my heart become light." And by verbal sleight of hand, the heart *is* light.

But it does not stop there. In the next line, you pick up what you transformed once and transform it once again. "May that light glow like stars." And now, indeed, we see stars. You continue this way until you have finished with your wishes, then end by repeating the first important word: "May . . . become my heart." Once the circle has been closed, the magic begins.

The formula for the charm, then, is as follows:

May *a* become *b*
May *b* become *c*
May *c* become *d*

> May *d* become *f*
>
> May *f* become . . .
>
> May . . . become *a*.

You do not need to use rhyme, although rhyming makes for pleasant charms, as the example in the next section will show you. You can also vary the line length and sentence structure, so long as you keep the pattern intact.

You can create healing charms for almost any intention: to become happier, to grow healthier or stronger, to pass a test, to attract love. Be sure to ask yourself what it is you really desire. If you do not believe you are loveable, attracting a handsome lover will only backfire. Because you will not feel worthy of love you might withdraw, become possessive, or otherwise find ways to prove yourself right. It is far better to work toward healing your own sense of inadequacy than to cast a charm over someone else.

Instead of bewitching others, work magic on yourself. Do you know the meaning of the word "glamour"? A Celtic word (from Scottish Gaelic), it means a spell that makes something appear more desirable than it really is. Do you want mere glamour, or do you want the reality? Heal yourself from any inner wounds or lack of self-confidence, and the light you emanate will attract the right people to you.

## An Example of a Healing Charm

Here is an example of a healing charm. Notice how the charm is formed: each linked image is transformed into the next, and into the next, and finally the circle is closed at the end. You may also notice how you can play with the form to create interesting variations. This is a charm for personal beauty:

> My body is a rose; may she bloom.
> My bloom is fragile as a flower
> that brightens in a sunlit hour
> and fades when sunlight's gone.

My spirit is the sun; may she shine.

My shining is the fragrance of the rose

that tells us everything the flower knows

and shows its beauty even to the blind.

My beauty is my own: may I know it.

My beauty is the rose within my youth.

My beauty is my body's rosy truth.

My beauty is for all; may I show it.

About cursing: while it is sometimes tempting, when angry, to try to cast a curse or hex upon someone, be careful about giving in to such temptation. There is power in words, and it can as easily loop back to hit you in the face as find its intended target. In contemporary Wicca, the "rule of three" is sometimes invoked. This says that whatever you send out will come back to you, strengthened three times. Concentrate on strengthening yourself with healing charms rather than using verbal magic to attack others.

## Activities for Healing Wild Girls

 Perform a mirror ritual. Set up a mirror so that you can look into it comfortably. Put a candle beneath or next to it, and light it. Then look into your face in the mirror. Look into your own eyes. As you do so, imagine that you are giving yourself unconditional love. Do not let any negative or critical thoughts intrude on this sacred moment. When you have finished, blow out the candle while wishing yourself a good morning or evening.

 Make a self-confidence alphabet: for each letter of the alphabet, write one word that describes your best qualities. Write the alphabet in a tiny booklet and illustrate it with cut-out flowers. Put the booklet under your pillow and picture the positive words filling your dreams as you sleep.

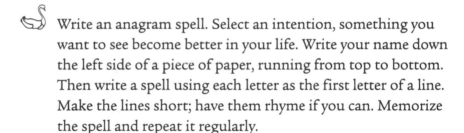 Write an anagram spell. Select an intention, something you want to see become better in your life. Write your name down the left side of a piece of paper, running from top to bottom. Then write a spell using each letter as the first letter of a line. Make the lines short; have them rhyme if you can. Memorize the spell and repeat it regularly.

Take a healing bath. Take an hour or so for this ritual; do not rush. Fill a bathtub with warm water and pleasant-smelling bath oil or bubble bath. Before you get in, rub your body thoroughly with a mixture of almond oil and Epsom salt. Then light a candle, lower the lights, and enter the tub. As you float there dreamily, imagine the water being a substance that will bring health, vitality, and joy to every cell in your body.

Create a healing altar. Make a list of places, people, colors, objects, times of the year—anything that makes you feel safe and happy when you think of it. Then find those objects or representatives of them: a photo of autumn trees, or a fallen leaf; a piece of lace from grandmother; a bright-colored scarf. Use these objects to create a healing altar. Write a chant for yourself, a small, easy-to-remember poem that mentions your healing objects and people. Read or recite it daily for a month in front of the healing altar.

# 6

# *Who Brought Endless Winter to the Land?*

## Pacific Northwest

**O**nce, not so very long ago, winter came and stayed. On the frozen river, ice did not move. Beneath the ice, the water was empty. Fish lived there once, but all had been caught and eaten.

There was hunger in the tents of the people. Spring winds did not warm the land. The days did not grow longer.

Each morning, as the sun rose late into the sky, the village elders looked at each other and wondered when spring would finally come. Mothers dug all day in the snow, looking for the only food they could find: twigs and dry leaves. Pounded together, it tasted like sawdust or medicine, but even that tastes good to hungry people.

The children were very, very hungry. The elders, counting the days, knew it was June. But snow stood on the ground next to the ice-locked river. At night, wild winds tore at the leather tents, while inside children nestled deeper into their fur blankets, trying to ignore the pain in their stomachs.

In July, there was still as much ice and snow as in December. At last a council was called. It was held in the home of the oldest woman. One by one the elders entered through the short flap of the tent, arranging themselves in a ring around the tiny fire.

"What," asked the oldest elder, "has caused winter to remain these long months in our land?"

They all fell silent, staring into the fire and into their memories. Something, they knew, must have upset the spirits of earth. Something had caused this punishment to come upon them. But what?

The elders sat with their fur blankets wrapped around them. Their dark eyes closed as they concentrated on the problem. Here and there an already-wrinkled forehead wrinkled even more in a frown.

An hour passed in silence. Then an old voice croaked, "Bird murder."

The elders did not stir, but their eyes travelled to the old man who had spoken.

"An endless winter results from the needless killing of a bird."

Slowly, the elders began to relax. They looked at each other, nodding slightly. Yes, that was it. It happened so rarely that none remembered the last incident, but all had heard the story, dim years ago, in their youth.

Someone in the village had murdered a bird. The only way to bring spring was to find that person.

One by one, each member of each family was called forward. Each told the elders, "I killed no bird except for food." First came the hunters: none of them had committed the crime. None of the mothers admitted to it. One by one, the children said they did not do it. Each one said the necessary words, "I killed no bird except for food." Finally, one girl blurted, "I killed no bird except for food—but Wakanee did! I saw her!"

The elders looked somberly at each other. Wakanee was a bright-eyed girl, the only child of her parents. She was called in to the elders' council. Crying, she admitted the crime. "I did not mean to do it!" she tried to explain. "I was throwing rocks and one of them hit a bird and it died."

Wakanee's family stiffened with sorrow. Her father looked sadly at his wife. Wakanee's mother clenched her fists but said nothing, either to her daughter or to the elders.

Wordlessly, the parents left the tent, returning a few moments later with Wakanee's best clothing, a pair of soft moccasins embroidered with porcupine quills, a warm leather skirt and an overblouse fringed with beads. These were her holiday clothes but Wakanee, tears running down her cheeks, knew that no holiday waited for her.

Someone began a chant as mournful as the winds that tugged at the leather tents each night. Wakanee's parents pulled the girl's beautiful holiday clothes onto her. She did not resist.

Then, one at a time, the people walked to the riverbank, across the crunching snow. Wakanee's mother walked unspeaking beside her daughter.

At the riverbank where snow met ice, one of the elders approached Wakanee and put his hands on her shoulders. Everyone bowed. Tears trickled from the corners of many eyes.

Wakanee had stopped crying. She was too scared to cry. She did not know what was going to happen to her, but she was afraid. She stood tense and pale under the heavy hands of the elder.

The elder raised his hands and eyes. He pointed out onto the ice. Wakanee did not understand. She stood still, staring at the old man. He pointed again, saying nothing. Wakanee realized that he meant her to walk on the river ice. She had seen people walking on the frozen river all winter. It did not scare her. So she started walking.

The river was very wide at that point. It took many moments for Wakanee to reach the center. When she did, she turned and looked back at the small knot of people gathered on the river bank. She began to raise her hand to wave at them.

A sudden slamming sound, and in an instant spring arrived. Ice rushed out of the river, carried on fierce currents. And Wakanee too was carried, away from the people gathered on the shore.

In the village, snow melted all at once and ran down to the river in a flood. Birds arrived in a rush of singing. Trees budded and broke into leaf, all in an instant. From empty soil flowers sprang up and blossomed.

The transformation from winter into July took but a moment. The villagers stood gasping, stunned and entranced by the speed of summer's coming. The children ran into the woods, laughing, to gather strawberries.

Wakanee's mother walked slowly home, her husband at her side. They saw the justness of their daughter's punishment. They were glad for the others that there was again food to eat. But they grieved, for they had no other children. They would grow old alone.

Summer passed peacefully, though the village missed the bright neighbor who had disappeared in the crashing ice. The rivers were full of salmon. The people caught more than enough for the winter, hanging some to dry, storing the precious oil in big wooden boxes. There were many berries—fat huckleberries, blueberries the size of pebbles, juicy raspberries. There was enough food for two winters. The people gathered what they needed and stored some away against harder times.

Winter came late that year, as if to make up for staying so long the last time. And when it came, it came slowly. Winds from the sea blew cold into the village for many weeks before the mountaintops turned white. And that snow—late as it was in coming—did not last many months. It scarcely seemed that a season had passed before spring arrived again.

The river tugged at its icy cover and broke into chunks. Drifting seaward, the icebergs melted. Sometimes a particularly big iceberg passed close to shore, and those in the village grinned, glad to see so much of winter disappearing at once.

One day, however, a block of river ice, travelling swiftly down the river, caught on the exposed root of a huge cedar near the village. It caused a great stir, for when the people came down to push it off with poles, they saw the body of Wakanee frozen within it.

The girl's body should have been carried out to sea the previous winter. No one could explain why it was there, going the wrong way through the waters. But they hacked away the ice and pulled the girl's body to shore, then carried it in ceremony back to the village. She was, after all, a heroine. The girl had died to save her village. Her crime, they knew, had been unintentional, but nonetheless she had suffered terribly for it.

Hardly had they brought the body back to the village, however, than a pink flush crept into Wakanee's cheek. Her mother ran out of the tent toward her daughter. Wakanee gave a great sigh, the sound of breath going into lungs empty for more than a year. Then she opened her eyes.

Looking up, she saw villagers staring down at her. She pulled herself to one elbow and took another deep breath. From every corner of the little village, people were running to see her. She sat up, then stood.

When she spoke, it was to the eldest in the village. The old man who had sent her onto the ice had died the previous winter, and this woman was now oldest of the elders. "Grandmother," she said, "I have returned."

The old woman nodded her head.

"I have learned much that will be of use," Wakanee said.

The old woman nodded again.

"I must have a tent of my own and a hunter to hunt for me," Wakanee finished.

The woman nodded yet again, then looked across the circle of villagers to a young man, a good hunter. She nodded at him, then at Wakanee. "Take care of it," she said.

Wakanee lived out her life as a sacred being, for she understood the ways of winter and read its signs. When the sky blew full of dark, thin clouds, she could tell if the snow was coming or would pass over. She knew the depth of ice from its blueness, the strength of river ice beneath moccasined feet, the places snow hid winter berries. When the days lengthened, she could tell if winter was going to go quickly or hang on through early spring.

Most of all, she understood the language of birds. When the geese skeined above, heading north to their nesting lands or south for winter warmth, she listened to their discussions of the weather. She spoke to sparrows, learning where juicy berries could be found. Even the owls conversed with her, sharing their great wisdom.

All the secrets of winter Wakanee knew, for winter had made her its daughter that terrible year. All the secrets of the bird people Wakanee knew for, having paid for her crime against them, they adopted her as one of their own. And so she lived, among yet not one of her people, sharing with them her hard-won wisdom.

• • •

# Goddesses of the Pacific Northwest

Thousands of years ago, the rainy Pacific Northwest coast of the American continent was settled by people who loved that land for its bounty and richness. Great cedar trees provided fuel and building materials for handsome, decorated homes. Bears, our distant relations, wandered the hills, providing food for brave hunters. Salmon swarmed through the wide rivers every year, bringing food and oil inland. There was plenty to hunt—moose and deer, squirrel and geese. There was plenty to harvest—berries and mushrooms and wild grains. People lived well and happily.

Because the land was so rich, there was room for many nations in the area: Bella Coola, Haida, Tlinget, Tshimshian, Okanagan, Nez Pierce, and many others. Their religions included many powerful goddesses, like Tacoma, the fierce and jealous mountain goddess after whom the great volcano is named; Gyhldeptis, the forest mother whose hair hangs like moss from the trees; and Rhpisunt, the ancestral mother who married a bear and bore half-bear children. Although cultures and customs varied widely throughout what we now call the states of Washington and Oregon and southeast Alaska, and the province of British Columbia, the varying nations shared a belief that it was important not to waste the natural bounty of their lands.

Like many of America's original residents, the Chinook who told the story of Wakanee had stern rules against being wasteful or careless of the lives of other beings. In this traditional tale, a girl is punished when starvation visits her people. There is a happy ending, but only after Wakanee has learned how to live gracefully and carefully among the other creatures of the earth. She is provided with gifts after she has learned this lesson. This story is one of the many told around the world in ancient times that were designed to remind us that we are not alone on this earth and that we must honor our neighbors, the plants and animals that some Native Americans called simply "all our relations."

## Our Place on Earth

Saturday afternoon, and you drive down to the mall. It's warm there in winter, cool in summer, so you can wear what you like. While driving, you call some friends on your cell phone to meet you there. When you get there, you drink a soda and eat some corn chips, throwing away the cup and wrappers. You buy a new pair of earrings, even though you have thirty pairs at home. You watch a movie with a lot of special effects, then go home in time for dinner. You check your purse before you leave. Good deal! You're only out $25. Not bad.

But if you could count the cost of everything, what was the *real* price of your day at the mall? What did it cost the earth to produce the corn, and what will it cost the soil to eliminate the toxins in the pesticide the farmers used? What will it cost the air to absorb the heavy metals that the mall's power plant exhales? What will it cost the oceans to eliminate the wastes our sewage systems carry out to sea?

And what of the social costs? What does it cost the Asian woman, only a few years older than you, who has to leave her small children to work for low wages, making the earrings you bought? What does it cost the farmer forced to sell a family farm because of the cost of artificial fertilizer? What do the roads and water systems cost that support the mall?

Nothing, our wise ancestors knew, is unconnected to anything else. When you turn up the heat instead of putting on a sweater, a network of changes ripples through the world. More fuel is burned at your local power plant, leading to more air pollution, bits of hard ash floating around like smog. A bird's migration route is altered when a wetland is filled with waste from the power plant. Far away, in the Arctic, a fox starves because birds do not arrive at the end of a long, cold winter. The death of that fox means a litter of little foxes is not born that summer, and so squirrels begin to multiply, unchecked by fox predation. An ancient forest begins to die away, and nothing grows to replace it because all the seeds have been eaten by the innumerable squirrels. Soil begins to wash into the sea, no longer held in place by the roots of trees.

How about that burger you had for lunch last week? Was the steer it was made from fed on corn harvested from genetically altered plants? These plants have been created in laboratories, their genes changed so that they emit their own pesticide. While this keeps the plants free of bugs, and therefore increases the harvest (and therefore the profit margin), the pollen from these unnatural plants drifts over to nearby blooming milkweed. There it poisons monarch butterflies, who feed largely on milkweed. Within twenty years, it is predicted, there will be no more monarch butterflies in the world. But we will have had many cheap burger lunches.

Our actions have consequences. Even our smallest actions. Even an accident or unintentional action can cause dramatic change.

But how could Wakanee's accident cause a prolonged winter? In physics, this is described as "sensitive dependence upon initial conditions." Science today has rediscovered some of the wisdom of our elders on this continent, especially the idea that we are interconnected in a web of life. Sometimes called the Butterfly Effect, this scientific theory tells us that a storm in California can be caused by a butterfly flapping its wings in China. Tiny waves of air set in motion by the butterfly can be amplified again and again until great gusts of wind result. If a tiny butterfly can have such an effect, why not the death of a bird? The absence of that one being, with all its activities and interconnections, could have similarly set in motion a series of consequences that resulted in endless winter.

How do we live in a world where everything is connected this way? We probably will not go back to living in tents and using wood for heat. But we can be thoughtful about our consumer habits. Why not refill a water bottle at home, rather than toss it and buy another? Why not refuse to buy cosmetics tested on animals, causing pain and death to helpless creatures? Why not curb spending for fun, trying to live with more awareness of the social and ecological costs of such behavior? Why not patronize shops and companies that attempt to promote a balanced way of living on the earth?

We are butterflies. Our smallest actions have effect. If we learn to take that seriously, we can feel our own power as well as our own responsibility for sustaining our blue planet.

## Finding Your Power Being

It is common, among people who live close to the earth, to believe that we each connect with a specific being—plant or animal or rock or place. Sometimes it is part of one's heritage, as with Australian "dreaming places," where the animal or insect ancestors of their family dwelled at the time of Creation. Sometimes the relationship is individual, as when young people find names and power beings in a "vision quest" among North America's Plains Indians. Some cultures believe we are tied to one being throughout our lives; others believe that different stages of our lives demand different beings that reveal themselves to us as needed.

Sometimes such beings are called "totem animals," though they might be fish or plants or insects rather than mammals. The word "totem" actually means the being that stands at the head of your ancestral line. In ancient times, people often bore the names of the animals from whom they descended. This was the case in many European as well as other nations. A name like Black Elk makes its totemic background clear, but what of McMurrow or Gruenwald? Just names, right? But the first is Irish for "child of the otter," the second is German for "greenwood," and both reveal the totem beings of the ancestral past.

In addition to ancestral totems, we often have personal totem (or power) beings. Sometimes these reveal themselves in dreams. As part of your exploration of the goddess path, you have been recording your dreams. Read through them to see if any animals appear regularly. Not all dream animals serve your spiritual quest as totem animals. Look for ones that appear as helpful beings or guides. The horse that carries you away from trouble, the friendly dog by your side, the emblem of a bear carved on the side of a building, a piece of jewelry in the shape of a raven—all can indicate a power animal revealing itself to you.

Waking dreams, too, offer you an opportunity to explore your personal symbolism and locate your power beings. To use this form of meditation, also called active imagination, find yourself a comfortable place to sit. If you have some simple drumming music, put it on; or if you have a friend who is willing to drum for you, have her set a simple steady beat and maintain it.

Make sure there's enough light that you do not doze off. Then, beginning with your toes, tense and relax all your muscles. Go slowly up your legs, over your torso, up your arms, and finally up the neck and face to the top of your head. Tighten the muscles, each in turn; hold them for a moment, then release. Once you have completed this exercise with all your muscles, you are ready to begin the quest for your power being.

Imagine a place where you feel safe and, with your inner eye, picture yourself there. Let yourself witness everything about the place. Use all your inner senses: see, hear, taste, smell, and touch everything. Once you have made this sacred inner space as real as the outer world, find an opening leading out of the space. It could be a stairway; it could be a tree you climb; it could be a stone you overturn to find a hole beneath.

Notice whether the opening leads up or down as you follow the path that opens out from it. Imagine yourself moving through this space. Observe everything: colors, fragrances, temperatures, everything. Continue moving in this new space until you find a place to stop.

Wait there, in this inner space. Just notice what is around you. After some time—the length of time varies with each individual—you will notice some being in the space. It might enter, or it might have been there all along, trying to catch your attention. In your inner body, approach this being and greet it. You might bow or wave, speak or make contact only with your inner eyes. Notice how the being responds. It might move, or speak, or offer you something. When you believe the encounter over, thank your inner guide and retreat. Go back along the route to the safe space you originally occupied, and then slowly come back to waking consciousness.

Do not share your experience with anyone else until you have written it down or drawn it out. When you have done so, you may find no need to tell anyone about it. Your power being is your precious connection to nature; no one else needs to know about it. However, if you have spiritually minded friends or a Wild Girls' Circle, you may choose to discuss the experience with them. Be careful when you do that you remain always aware that a power being is a gift to you, not something to claim or brag about. A grasshopper can be a more significant power being than a wolf, if the person relates to it correctly. There is no "right" or "wrong," no "better" or "worse," with power beings. If you are given one, you are blessed.

If you do not encounter a power being on your first expedition to your inner wilderness, do not be concerned. You may not be ready to meet your power being, or you may have met it without realizing it. Many people discover, over the course of their lives, several power beings who make themselves available when the need arises. Journey regularly to your inner spaces, and you will encounter all the powers you need there.

## Omens and Divination

A skill related to finding power beings is that of reading omens. In ancient times, omens were a part of every day. Some of these were direct observations of the natural world around us. Even today, some navigators among Pacific Islanders are able to detect storms days in advance by careful attention to changes in the wind and the ocean's color. This can seem like magic to someone who does not observe these subtle natural phenomena. Other omens are events in the outer world that somehow correspond to our inner world. Several kinds of such omens are listed below.

> **Things out of place:** A book lying on a park bench; a playing card carried by the wind to your feet; a misdelivered package; anything not in the place where you would expect it to be.

> **Things at the wrong time:** A grandfather clock chiming twelve times at 6 A.M.; a rose blooming in snow; a birthday card that arrives months late; anything that occurs at an unanticipated time.

> **Words out of nowhere:** A meaningful phrase that appears on a billboard; a name that you overhear several times; a significantly misspelled word; any word that repeats itself or appears out of place.

> **Repeating images:** A place that appears several times in conversation, on television, in pictures; an image from a dream that you see

in waking life; a bird that flies by just as you are reading about birds; any unusual repetitions or echoes.

Interpreting omens is not easy. You might find books that offer you lists of meanings for various omens—but these are limited, because your own meaning might differ from what is published. Never use just one source for omen interpretation, no matter how good it may appear. To interpret an omen, investigate all the potential meanings of the image or word. Use dictionaries, mythic encyclopedias, glossaries of symbolism, your own dreams and associations—compile all of them without trying to select only the positive meanings. It is often easier to interpret others' omens than our own; who is really honest with herself when it comes, for instance, to love? Ask for help from your Wild Girl friends. In all cases, do not let any omen interpretation push you to actions you feel uneasy about.

## Activities for Earth-loving Wild Girls

 Examine your last name and the names that appear in your family tree. Look up their meanings in a foreign-language dictionary from the country of your origin, if the names are not already in English. Can you find one or more of your totem ancestors?

 Examine your first and middle names for their meanings. Look in dictionaries and other reference books until you are sure you have found all possible meanings. Examine what other relatives have your names. Are there images or totems hidden in your names?

 Make a power shield. Cut a round piece of cardboard (or beg a spare from a pizza kitchen) and divide it into four quadrants. Label the quadrants north, south, east, and west—the "four quarters" of the visible universe. In the east, color or paint power in images of air, however you experience it. In the west, put water; in the south, fire; in the north, earth. Color each quadrant in colors you associate with those elements; draw, stamp, or paste images that fill you with those elemental powers.

 Go on an amulet hike. Fill your pocket with silver coins, bits of broken jewelry, or other things you will not mind leaving behind. Select a natural area like a park or forest or beach; go alone or with others, but if you travel with others, do so silently so that the objects around you may speak to you. Allow at least an hour for this hike. Walk through the natural area, looking carefully at each and every rock, plant, and other resident. Some—not many—will volunteer to go home with you. If you find something that truly calls to you, offer the earth something in return for it. Take as little as you possibly can: a petal rather than an entire flower, a leaf rather than a branch. Make sure you leave things undisturbed as you pass, and pick up any litter you encounter. When you return from the hike, put the object or objects on your altar and ask for guidance in accepting its power.

 Have a giveaway. Go through all your possessions and make a pile of everything you never use: clothing you've outgrown, books you read long ago, jewelry you never did wear. Be ruthless—if you have not worn something in two years, you probably are not going to wear it again. Next, locate places to donate the still-useful objects. Throw nothing away that still could be used by someone. Shelters for battered families or homeless people are always in need of useful materials; a local civic organization may have a campaign for the less fortunate. As you give away your excess, thank from your heart the person who accepts it from you.

## 7

# *By the Fountain at the Edge of the Sky*

## Baltic

**E**ven in heaven, not all families are happy. Even in heaven, some daughters keep sad secrets from their mothers. Some mothers are blind to their daughters's suffering. Even in heaven, some pain ends in separation, for no other ending is possible.

Along the shores of the white northern sea, in the lands of birch forests and tidy farms, ancient stories were once sung. The Balts, the people of Lithuania and Latvia, sang of the sun mother Saule and her star daughters. They sang of the earth's springtime, when the lovely sun first met the handsome moon.

*Saule met Meness*

*in the earth's springtime.*

*Saule was engaged*

*when the earth was still young.*

All the world was beautiful then. Earth had not yet aged and wrinkled into mountains. Green grasses covered gentle hills. The blue waters were fresh and pure. The air sparkled. Above this beautiful world, the sun and the moon danced joyously, holding hands, gazing into each others' eyes.

The earth sang with joy. The song formed itself into birds; it flowed through the air as soft winds. The song drifted through flowering trees, praising the sun goddess and the moon god. When Meness lifted from Saule's head her maiden-crown, the whole world was made of music.

Saule and Meness lived together in a little house on the edge of the sky. From Earth you could see them next to each other: the radiant sun and her husband, sitting side by side on the horizon. Young men and young women, seeing how happy life could be, took each other by the hand and walked smiling through the world.

They traveled together across the sky every day. Saule drove her chariot beside her husband, trimming forests with her golden scissors as she passed. She watched over the world, guiding home lost travellers and helping those in need. When, each night, they reached the western gates of the world, Saule watered her tired horses, then threw open the doors of heaven to welcome all who had died that day. After a great feast in the red sunset, night fell.

Saule and Meness had many children. Saule loved them all, but her favorite was her oldest daughter, Austrina. As Saule arrived each night, she always looked for Austrina. And her daughter was always there to greet her. It was Austrina who sat with Saule each evening in front of the fire. It was Austrina who sang her mother to sleep each night.

This was the happy heaven of long ago. On Earth, too, people lived without war or violence. All was peaceful, full of beauty. It was the earth's best time, the time we only visit now in dreams.

But it is all lost now. Lost, except for peaceful dreams.

One fateful morning, Meness had stayed at home. He had begun to stay at home many mornings, saying Saule's light would be sufficient for the world. As she moved across the sky, Saule sensed that something was wrong, like a cloud's shadow or a gray veil across the day's radiance. Her horses pulled the sun chariot smoothly across the sky, the day was bright and beautiful, and nothing seemed wrong on earth. But still, Saule sensed something amiss. She watched everything beneath her with such care that it was a weary goddess who reached heaven that evening.

Austrina was not there. Saule was surprised. She called to her daughter as she tied up her brown horses. "Austrina!" she called. "Where is my white lily? Where is my daughter?"

There was no reply.

Never, in all the endless years of heaven, had Austrina failed to meet her mother at sunset. Cold gripped the sun's heart. She searched the palace and its gardens. Was she in the kitchen, making supper? No. In the laundry, shaking out the white sheets of clouds? Not there. In her bedroom, asleep or sick? No, not there either.

Saule called her daughter's name so loudly the heavens shook. No one answered. Saule asked everyone she met in heaven's halls. No one had seen Austrina.

Frantic, Saule ran into the garden. No one was there!

But wait . . . at the far end . . . down by the little fountain . . . was that a white dress?

Saule ran down the path, calling her daughter's name. "There you are . . ." Saule began, but her voice stopped when she saw her daughter's face.

At first Saule thought Austrina was crying. No: there was no red around her eyes, no flushed cheeks. Yet something had changed in her daughter's face.

"What has happened?" Saule demanded.

"Nothing." Austrina kept her eyes cast down. She examined a little golden ring she wore. Every once in awhile she twisted it on her finger.

"Nothing?" said the sun goddess. "Then why are you in the garden when I've just come home?"

Austrina slowly got up. "Sorry," she said. "I forgot."

The sun goddess smiled. She thought of how she had felt as a young girl. The trees had seemed so full of flowers then, and sometimes the garden pathways seemed to wind deeper every moment. She looked at her daughter with understanding.

Or so she thought. But Saule did not, in fact, understand. She could not, for what had happened to Austrina was new to the world—new, and terrible beyond speaking.

After that, day after day, Saule returned with her star-spangled horses to find Austrina sitting by the fountain, or by the fire, or in her bedroom. Austrina no longer spun the balls of fine silk that her mother unwound across the sky into sunlight. She no longer wove beautiful tapestries of light. She no longer met the handsome twin gods when they came calling.

She simply sat, twisting her golden ring around her finger, slowly, slowly. And she did not speak.

Saule was patient. She teased her daughter sometimes. But mostly she just let her alone. She thought Austrina was lost in awareness of her coming womanhood. From her chariot in the sky, the sun goddess saw everything on earth, but Saule did not see what happened in her own palace—in her own bedroom—when she was away.

One day the sky road was shorter than usual. Perhaps the heavenly horses were faster than usual. Or perhaps Perkuna Tete, great lady of thunder, worked magic to get Saule home early. However it happened, the sun set half an hour early one night. Saule entered her palace and found no one to greet her.

Sighing, tired, she walked toward her bedroom.

As she reached for the door, it opened. Meness the moon man came out. He looked surprised. Without speaking, he ran past Saule, out toward the stable. Saule heard him call for his white horses and his crescent chariot.

Saule entered the room. To her surprise, she found Austrina, lying under the bedcovers. Her face was vacant, her eyes half-closed.

Fearing illness or worse, Saule ran to her.

As Saule reached the bed, Austrina's naked shoulders rose from the sheets. In a sickening flash, the sun goddess realized what had happened. She stooped for only a moment to kiss her daughter. Then she was gone.

In the stable, Meness had hitched the moon horses and was on his way out heaven's doorway. But he proved too slow. At the edge of heaven, Saule met him, a huge silver sword stretched above her head. "Stop!" she commanded. But Meness rode the moon chariot as fast as he could, right past the sun goddess.

She swung at him as he passed. The flat blade of the silver sword hit one cheek, then the other. Still Meness did not stop. Bleeding, he fled into the sky.

Instantly, Saule closed the sky gate. He would never again enter her home and hurt her daughter. The peace of heaven was shattered—forever. But her daughter would be safe from the treacherous moon.

Saule ran back to her bedroom. Austrina was gone! But this time, the sun goddess knew where to look.

Down at the garden fountain, the sun goddess found her daughter. Austrina's hand drooped into the magical waters. She seemed oblivious to everything: the blossoming trees, the brightening stars, her mother. She sang a little song to herself:

> *Where, oh where, O mother mine,*
> *Shall I wash my white robe?*
> *Where shall I wash out the blood?*

Tears coursed down Saule's face, turning into golden amber as they fell. For a moment, she hesitated. Did her daughter hate her for learning too late how the moon had hurt her? Could she ever win her daughter's love again?

But love overcame caution. Saule walked to Austrina and reached strong arms around her. She pulled off her blue cloak and wrapped it around her daughter.

For a moment, all was still. Austrina did not move. Her soft singing ceased. Even the birds were silent. The wind sang no melodies in the garden's flowery trees.

Then, very slowly, like a flower opening, Austrina turned to her mother. And, very softly, she began to cry.

For days they sat there, mother and daughter, weeping. Their sadness seemed endless. They wept for lost innocence and beauty and joy. They wept for what had been done, what could not be undone.

On earth, people cried out in fear. The sun did not rise. The earth grew cold. Wars broke out. Families were torn apart by violence. What had happened in heaven?

When the sun finally rose, it was to a different world. Saule's people looked up, joyous at the return of their goddess. But look! No moon husband stood beside her. Only a lovely star, never before seen, burned through the dawn sky beside the sun.

Saule traveled the sky that day alone, her daughter hidden in the folds of her sunny cloak. But as the sun set that night, she came out to open the gates, and the people of earth saw her glowing softly in the purple evening. And then, an even greater surprise: when the moon man rose, his face was full of scars and blood. His chariot entered the sky as far as it could from Saule's departing horses.

And that is the way they are seen even today. Heaven's innocence is gone, but Meness the moon man can never touch his daughter again, for flaming Saule stands guard on heaven's gateway. But because of his crime, our world has changed forever. Daughters are no longer always safe, nor mothers at ease.

Earth's springtime has ended. In its place is the world we know, with its single blossoming season to remind us of what we have lost.

•   •   •

## Goddesses of the Baltic

On the shores of the Baltic Sea, on the northern edge of Europe, live the Lithuanians and the Latvians. They are related peoples, speaking one of the oldest European languages. They are renowned as miners and traders of amber, a precious sun-colored jewel found only in their lands and, in ancient times, worth more than gold. This was the land of the great sun goddess Saule, who drove her chariot through the sky each day and warmed the earth. She was the most important and best-loved divinity of her people, honored in song and story.

There were other goddesses of the Baltic. Laima, the fate goddess who predicted our life's course at birth. Jurate, the mermaid who lives with the prince of tides beneath the sea. Perkuna Tete, the thunder goddess. Milda, goddess of love songs. The tree goddess Egle, the snake goddess Aspelenie, the fertile earth-goddess Zemyna. All were honored in rituals that continued for millennia, until only a few hundred years ago when the Baltic area was converted to the new religion of Christianity. Some of the goddesses, christened as saints, continued to be honored under different names. Saule, the great sun goddess, became identified with mother Mary, and her amber-studded portraits can still be seen in Baltic lands and, in America, in Lithuanian and Latvian family homes.

Just as Saule was the center of heaven, so the mother was the center of the Baltic home. Women were highly regarded for their contributions to the family's wealth, especially for their hand-spinning and weaving, which provided all the thread and cloth for the nation. They were also the land's greatest poets, whose works are still treasured in their homeland. Of all the ancient Baltic poems, the most beautiful are those that praise a mother's love for her daughter and a daughter's love for her mother. In the archives in the Latvian capital of Riga and the Lithuanian city of Vilnius, millions of these poems are still to be found, testimony to the strength and beauty of the women of the Balts.

## Combating Negative Situations

How did evil come into the world? Every spiritual tradition has examined this important question. In some religions, a devil brings evil, tempting us to follow him; in other traditions, evil exists because good falls asleep and needs to be prodded awake; others say that evil exists so that we may grow compassionate toward each other, because none of us can be perfect. Because of war, violence, rape, murder, and other evils, spiritual traditions struggle with the question of how and why such evil exists.

People on the goddess path must also grapple with this problem. We cannot deny that there are negative influences on our lives as well as positive ones. How can we come to terms with this reality? How can we understand its lessons for our spiritual quest?

It would be nice to assume that young women lead happy lives untouched by evil, that only in later life is this question important. Unfortunately, this is far from true. Unfair teachers, prejudiced classmates, economic hardships—these are just some of the problems that girls face on a daily basis. But such hurts are dealt by those outside the family, so parents and children can struggle together against them. How many poor families have raised children who win scholarships and become community leaders? How many families have offered a safe haven for girls when classmates or teachers have rejected them for the color of their skin, for their appearance, for their ideas? Painful as such rejections are, if there is support within the family, a young woman can endure and even thrive.

Violence and other evils within the family present a far greater spiritual challenge. Parents who abuse drugs or alcohol, parents who are physically abusive, parents who are verbally cruel, parents who sexually assault their children—these are unfortunately found in every community, every race and religion, every economic strata. Behind carefully tended lawns, behind bright-curtained windows, many girls live with danger and depression and pain as their daily companions.

When someone we love and depend on hurts us, it is especially difficult to know how to protect and defend ourselves. Like Austrina in the Baltic story, girls often withdraw into silence. It becomes easy to imagine that all families act the same way—that all fathers drink too much, all mothers entertain too many boyfriends, all brothers demand sex of their sisters. It becomes easy to become blind to abuse, to believe that it is just part of life.

Even worse, girls may blame themselves for the abuse they suffer. "If only I had kept my mouth shut," a girl will say, "he wouldn't have hit me." Another might say, "If only I do not look sexy, he will leave me alone." Or another, "If only I can keep the house clean enough and the kids quiet, maybe mom won't drink tonight." In an attempt to control the hurt and pain she endures, a girl may starve herself or eat too much; she may become verbally cruel or excessively timid; she may run away or never leave home. All of these, and many more behaviors, are responses to the confusion of love and hurt that girls can encounter within their families.

In the Baltic story above, we are reminded of a deep and wise secret of the goddess path. It is that no girl, alone, can combat family violence or evil. She needs help. In the story, Saule discovers what is happening and rushes to her daughter's rescue. In real life, unfortunately, many mothers are unable or unwilling to risk opposing a cruel father; or the mother herself may cause a girl pain and suffering. Therefore it is important to find other women— teachers, ministers, counselors, neighbors—who can help when the family becomes a hurtful place rather than a secure one. There are many women, and men as well, who can play the part of Saule, offering protection to the wounded daughter. A Wild Girl reaches out, bravely, knowing that there are those who care for her and can help protect her.

Parents and children often disagree about family life—how late to stay up or out, when homework must be done, whether a fashion is appropriate, and so forth. Learning to work through such disagreements is part of growing up, both for parents and for children. But no girl need endure physical violence or sexual assault within her own home. Any parent who tells a girl otherwise is lying. Part of the path of the young goddess is learning how to protect yourself and how to reach out for healing if you are hurt.

106

## Casting a Protective Circle

When we are hurt by someone we love and trust, we often shatter into pieces. The hurt goes into one part of the soul, the love into another. Otherwise, reality is too difficult to understand. Why would a parent hurt a child? How can we love someone who hurts us? It can drive us crazy, trying to make sense of such an impossible reality. So we put up walls to separate our conflicted feelings. The pain grows less. We get by, from day to day.

Unfortunately, this strategy means that we lose touch with who we really are. When part of our experience is denied, the part of us connected to that experience is drowned. We become less than our full selves. Very often, too, we find ways to act out our emotions in ways we think are safe. We cannot strike back at a parent, but we may create arguments with schoolmates in order to yell out our fury. When someone abuses our bodies and we cannot strike back at them, we can turn upon ourselves physically, cutting or starving or otherwise hurting ourselves.

Whether they experience danger at home or not, all girls on the path of the young goddess must learn to protect themselves—physically, emotionally, and spiritually. Martial arts, like karate and tae kwon do, are excellent ways to connect body, mind, and spirit. Wild Girls need to know how to protect themselves from assault by strangers. Hiding at home is no option; every year we hear news reports of girls hurt by strangers who break into their homes. Physical strength and agility also help empower girls who suffer from violence at home.

And every Wild Girl needs to know how to protect herself emotionally and spiritually. It is important to remember, in creating protective rituals, that you may not be able to control the abuse another heaps upon you. What you can control is your own reaction. You may not be able to stop a parent from hitting you, but you can protect your spirit sufficiently that, twenty years later, you do not mistake violence for love.

You do not have to endure painful experiences to need protection. You might wish to protect yourself against envy of your intelligence, or against hurtful slurs about your height. Social injustice that affects you can also demand protective rituals; prejudice against you because of race, color, appearance, weight, religion, or any other reason can corrode your self-esteem if you eat it as your daily diet. Protective rituals can assist you in surviving such negative influences.

To create a protective ritual, first sanctify the space you will use. Refer to chapter 1 for suggestions on creating a sacred space within which you can call for assistance in surviving hurt. On your altar, put some symbols of happier times: photographs, toys, and other mementos. Or use emblems of power from the natural world: stone, if you wish to be strong; seeds, if you wish to remember your creative potential; feathers, for the ability to fly above your troubles.

Sit or stand in your sacred space. Let yourself grow silent. Listen to your breathing. Imagine the billions of atoms that pass into and out of your body with each breath. Some are atoms that ancient priestesses breathed. Some are atoms from distant stars. We are, through each breath, connected with all time and all space, connected in that single sacred moment. Breathe for at least ten minutes, clearing your mind of anything but the powerful connection you make, through your breath, with the universe.

When you have centered yourself through breathing, imagine a globe of light around you. Imagine it forming an invisible barrier between yourself and the world. Within that globe, you are safe and whole. Visualize the globe glowing and pulsing. Within that glowing light, wrap your arms around yourself. Swing back and forth, as though you were rocking a baby. If you feel a need to cry, do so, for you are there to comfort yourself. If you need to scream (and are in a space where it is safe to do so), scream; or visualize yourself screaming while you hold yourself tight. Whatever emotions come forth, accept them. They are not unspiritual or wrong; they just are.

When you have experienced all the emotions connected with the pain you are enduring, quiet yourself again. Meditate upon the globe of light that surrounds you. Visualize the outside of the globe as a door that you can open, letting the outside in, or close, keeping negative influences away. Before you conclude your meditation, call to mind all those who can assist you in surviving the difficulties you encounter. Especially if you are enduring violence or abuse in your home, make a promise to yourself to locate people who will help you. If you cannot think of anyone you personally know, promise yourself that you will find a telephone hotline (see page 216) or Internet link that will put you in touch with those who can help. Your globe of light can help protect you, but you need never be alone.

Use this meditation any time you have been hurt. It is not a good idea to try it while someone is hurting you. Retreating to your sacred space at such times can create emotional blocks within yourself that can be difficult to undo later. Instead, use your martial arts, your verbal skill, or other people's help to try to get away or to change the situation. And if, despite all your efforts, you are hurt again, repeat your protective ritual again as soon as possible. Look for help as soon as you can. You need never be alone in your struggles and pain.

# Healing Rituals

Because hurt is inevitable in human life, all spiritual paths offer healing ceremonies to help knit up the brokenness within us. Those who walk the goddess path create their own ceremonies of healing. These ceremonies can be simple or complicated; they can take a few minutes or an hour; they can be done alone or with others. As you become aware of your own healing energy, you will be able to create rituals for whatever purpose you require. Here are some suggestions for starting the process. Although body, emotions, and spirit are actually a unity, it is easier to learn healing rituals by separating them. Later you may wish to create rituals that deal with multiple aspects of the self at once.

## Healing the Body

When you are sick, you probably employ common healing rituals such as taking medicine or drinking lots of fluids. Yes, these acts have scientific reasons for their effects. But science also knows something called the "placebo effect," in which people given identical but useless pills often experience healing simply because they expect to. Whenever you need physical healing, avoid just taking medicine and waiting passively for its effect. Instead, intentionally call upon your body's inner healing power as you use the medicine or other treatments you have been given. Similarly, establish some regular rituals to maintain your health. Outdoor exercise and good nutrition can be part of your spiritual path, too.

## Healing the Emotions

It is not possible to live a life without emotional upheaval. Our human task is to learn from conflict and difficulty, not to try to avoid it entirely. Whenever you find yourself emotionally upset by an experience, create a healing ritual by meditating upon the experience. Ask yourself what other times you have felt the same emotions. How is the new experience like earlier ones? What did you do to respond to the earlier occasions? How successful was that action? You are likely to find that you repeat your reactions to emotional situations. But if it did not work before, why should that action work now? When you have learned what your usual response has been, try something else. This way, although you will continually face new challenges in life, you will have healed yourself of making foolish mistakes again and again.

## Healing the Spirit

When you have been emotionally or physically hurt, your spirit has also been hurt. To begin to heal the spiritual wounds that earlier hurts have caused, think back to a period like the Golden Age in the story of Austrina, a time before the wounds were inflicted. Locate that memory in time and place. Then find a tiny memento of that time, or create a small image of it. Put the object in a little circle of pretty fabric and tie a ribbon or thread around it, enclosing it like a pouch. Carry or wear this amulet always; touch it whenever you feel your spiritual pain, and recall to mind that earlier, uninjured self.

## Activities for Protective Wild Girls

 Take a martial arts class. You should be able to find a karate, kickboxing, or similar program in your area. Check park districts, dance centers, community schools, and other facilities. Stop by and see a class in action before you sign up. Make sure you like the approach of the instructor; rely on your inner sense as to whether you find him or her trustworthy. Get a sister or friend to go with you to class, so that you can practice with each other; or go alone, and make a new friend who shares your interests there.

 Find a protective animal-totem. Using the instructions in chapter 6, journey to your inner wilderness and ask for a protector animal to appear. It may take one or more visits to your wilderness before you find what you need. Once you have met an animal protector, meditate on what wisdom the animal brings. A turtle, for instance, speaks of self-sufficiency; a bear of strength; a horse of being ready to run for your life. Find images of your protector—on jewelry, on fabric, in prints and pictures—and surround yourself with its power.

 Make a magical telephone list: list all the people you trust to come to your aid in a time of crisis. If you have difficulty making up such a list, work to locate one person who can assist you in reaching out for help when you need it. A women's center or community center is a good place to start. Relatives and older friends, too, can often offer help when you need it. Write the telephone numbers in small script on a piece of paper no more than two inches wide. Roll it up and sew it into a bracelet that you can wear when you feel you may need protection. Keep another copy of the list on your altar or in your spiritual diary (see chapter 9 for more ideas for your diary).

If you have been hurt by another, whether someone in the family or outside it, write down exactly what happened in your spiritual diary. Be as honest as you can be. Describe exactly what happened. When you believe you have written down everything, write down how you feel. If the situation happens again, follow the same directions: write down what happened, then how you feel. Do not show this diary to anyone. Keep it in a safe place.

 Tell your friends that you can be trusted to keep their secrets. If a friend tells you about a painful event, do not mention it to anyone. Wild Girls protect each other as well as themselves. If you have fallen into the habit of gossiping about other girls, realize that they may be suffering difficulties that make them seem strange to you. In your meditations, offer good thoughts to those whom you are tempted to mock. The understanding and compassion you offer them will come back to you when you need it.

# 8

# *The Girl Who Would Not Marry*

## Arctic North

Long, long ago, ice covered the world, so thick that even in summer, glaciers stood mountain-high above the tiny villages. In one of these, on a narrow spit of rocky shore next to an icy ocean, the girl Sedna lived with her father Anguta.

Her people lived a hard life. It was cold and dark half the year, and the air was filled with mosquitoes the other half. Food was scarce. There were birds to be caught in nets or brought down from the sky with stones. In spring, there were bird eggs. There were grasses and berries and roots. Gathering all of these was the work of women. So was catching small animals, like mice and rabbits, for the cooking pot.

The men were often away from the village, spending weeks tracking through treeless hills and over the icy rivers, hunting caribou and moose. A few times a year, they killed something. Then the taste of fresh meat and the stomach's fullness made everyone forget life's difficulties for a few hours.

That was all there was in this world to eat. The waters of the world were empty. The rivers ran, cold and clear, down to a lifeless sea. There were no fish or sea mammals. There was never a splash in the lake as a big pike jumped for a flying insect. There was never a vast sigh as a whale rose to breathe. Rivers did not throb with spawning salmon. And because there were no fish nor water mammals, animals and birds that now live on them—bear, gull, eagle—were scarce as well. The world was quiet and empty.

Gathering the scarce food filled Sedna's days. She was always busy, for her mother had gone away to live with a man in another village. Sedna did not miss her. Indeed, she barely remembered her. Sedna's father did not find a new wife. Instead he told his daughter to do her mother's work.

Anguta was a powerful hunter. He was gone most of the summer, and much of the winter too, hunting. So Sedna took care of herself.

She knew the seasons according to the food she gathered. In spring, she walked the hills slowly, looking for eggs. On lucky days, she'd fill a small basket with eggs of small birds. When she was even luckier, she found a goose nest and took one of the large brown eggs. She never took all the eggs from a single nest, knowing that some were needed to hatch a new generation of birds. No matter how much her stomach hurt with hunger, she left some food to grow into more food. Spring passed into summer. Lichen greened and dwarf berry bushes bloomed into tiny stars. Now there were herbs to be gathered, to be boiled in water and eaten green, or dried to flavor thin soup in the deep winter. The lengthening days passed in the rolling hills. Sedna set snares for rabbits and mice; she netted some birds. But often she went hungry.

As fall arrived, Sedna picked berries. A blueberry patch was a place to pass hours, fingers gripping every bright jewel. Crowberries were tiny black beads on delicate vines. Sometimes there were juicy cloudberries or bitter cranberries.

And then winter. Sedna could not gather food then, and lived off what she had stored and the dried meat her father brought home. But there were other tasks, chores that were necessary for warmth and survival. Leather had to be tanned by chewing and stretching animal skins. Boots had also to be made, and new parkas sewn. Every seam of every old garment had to be resewn, for it would be dangerous if a sleeve tore open on a bitter night and let in the killing wind. New baskets had to be woven for storage and cooking.

There was never a time when Sedna was not busy.

Sedna had taken over her mother's duties before she was seven. By the time she was twelve, old enough to marry, she was the best food provider the village had ever known. There were few girls in the village, and none so hardworking. Many boys looked at Sedna hopefully, for she was also round-faced and black-eyed, pretty to look at.

Sometimes a boy courted Sedna. He found her on the hills as she was gathering berries. Hiding behind a rock, he breathed a teasing poem at her:

> *Who can find*
> *rich bird eggs*
> *when they hide so deep*
> *in the marsh grass?*

An interested girl responded the same way. She pretended to talk about her work in little poems, but really teased the boy back. She would never say directly, to his face, that she liked a boy. No Eskimo girl would.

But Sedna did not peek at the boys and invent poems for them. She did not even speak. She ignored the boys, continuing her work as though no one else were there.

So no boys followed Sedna home to spend the evening in her father's house with her. Years passed. Other girls found husbands. Sedna's aloofness grew more obvious. At sixteen, she still showed no interest in marriage. The people of her village called her by a new name, a spiteful one. It meant "the girl who refuses to marry."

But she did not care. Her father was a good hunter. He might die on a hunting trip, but that could happen to a husband, too. He might grow too old to hunt. But that, too, could happen to a husband. So, for the time being, Sedna was content to spend her evenings staring at the white ocean. Endless and white, it reached to the horizon from the front of her small sod house. On its icy face, the winds arranged and rearranged delicate patterns. Even in the short summer, the wind moved the great water in mysterious designs.

But finally, even Sedna found love. One day in late summer, as she carried a basket full of cranberries home, Sedna stopped on the seashore to stare across the gray water. Winter was coming. There had been little food that year for women to gather. The hunters had poor luck, too. Perhaps people would starve that winter. Life could be terrible in the long darkness.

As Sedna stood by the seashore, she saw a small, moving shadow. It was a petrel, one of her favorite seabirds. It seemed almost to walk on the water as it swooped low across the ocean. Often she had stopped to watch the seabirds dance over gray water. This one seemed no different—at first.

As Sedna watched, the petrel came closer and closer. It also grew larger and larger. And Sedna realized it really *was* walking on the water!

The petrel walked right onto the beach. He nodded a greeting to Sedna. She was so amazed that she could not respond. It was as big as a man. Tawny feathers were sleek on its strong wings.

To Sedna's further astonishment, the bird spoke to her. Like a courting boy, he made up a riddle for her to answer.

*There is power*

*stronger than the sea wind*

*that can move a girl's heart.*

His voice sounded like wind in tundra grasses. Sedna put down her basket of berries. For the first time in her life, she replied.

*There is something*

*that lifts a girl*

*higher than her home,*

*higher than her father's home.*

The bird turned. Sedna climbed onto his back. Together they walked into the ocean. Sedna wrapped her arms around the petrel's neck and rested her cheek against his soft down. He lifted his huge wings and soared away.

As they travelled across the ocean, the petrel told Sedna that he was a prince of the sea. He said that he lived in a warm home filled with bearskins. He said he had plenty to eat. Sedna looked over her shoulders, once, to see the low hills retreating behind her. She might never see a human being again, but she was not the slightest bit sad.

They reached a tiny island far from shore. There the bird swooped down. Sedna dismounted. "Our home," the prince of petrels said, "is here."

The bird told Sedna that he had built a new home for her. He had watched her for years, he said. He loved her dignity and her hard work. It was time, the prince told Sedna, that she had someone to take care of her.

Sedna looked everywhere for the new home. Was it a sod house, as in her village? Or was it made of leather, a tent? She saw nothing except a huge, dirty bird's nest.

And that was where the petrel led her.

She had been promised bearskins, but there were just bits of bear hide. She had been promised food, but he gave her raw seaweed with some beetles now and then. It was the life of a petrel, not of a prince.

Sedna was disappointed, but she was a stubborn young woman. She had left her home with the bird, so Sedna settled down with the prince of petrels. She hid her anger and dismay as well as she could. But sometimes she stared out to sea in the direction of her father's land. She could see it for awhile, a dark line far across the water. Then winter came and the sea froze, and Sedna could see nothing but whiteness and the red ball of the sun for a few hours each day.

Sedna was cold all winter. The sea wind blasted from the ocean. The darkness lasted forever with no fire to break it.

Then, slowly, the sun returned to the north. But it did not bring much relief. Spring was bitter that year. The sea ice held fast and refused to melt. Finally summer came, but it was rainy. Sedna had never been so miserable.

Winter approached again. Sedna dreamed of escape. But how? She could not swim the icy ocean between the petrel's island and the shore.

But her father Anguta was a far-ranging hunter. During the summer, his travels had taken him near Sedna's island. Then, in autumn, he returned home the same way. From her seabird nest, Sedna recognized Anguta's kayak passing in the icy ocean beneath her. She shouted at him, her desperation causing her voice to carry farther than it usually did.

The keen-eared man heard the cry and recognized his daughter's voice. But hadn't she been kidnapped by spirits a year ago? Someone had seen her flying away on a cloud. He had missed her during the winter and had taken to hunting even in the worst weather.

There was nothing in sight except a rocky island with a huge bird's nest on it—nowhere for a girl to stay for a cold winter and a rainy summer. But Anguta could not deny the call. He paddled toward the rocky beach.

Sedna ran down to the shore to meet him. From the water he saw the familiar figure. Was it a spirit pretending to be his daughter, come to devour his soul? Anguta was no magician, but he knew that there were many levels of existence. There were evil spirits in the rocky islands, on the tundra, even around the village. They tried to trap the unwary with tricks like this.

Cautious as he was, Anguta could not resist the pleading in Sedna's voice. He pulled the kayak ashore. Father and daughter stared at each other as the chill wind pushed their parka fur into their faces. Their people did not show emotion, but both of them felt the joy of seeing each other once again.

"Father," she said somberly, "I ask you to take me to your home. My husband does not treat me well."

"A woman has the right to leave, then," said her father.

"I was courted with lies," she said. "My husband told me he was a prince. He said that I would live in plenty. But he is only a bird and feeds me seaweed and insects. I have no blankets against the cold. I have no leather to make clothes."

"There is no reason for a woman to be hungry and cold," Anguta agreed. "You shall come home."

"He will come after us," Sedna warned.

Anguta had killed many birds in his hunter's life. It did not trouble him to kill one more.

Sedna told him that, at evening, her husband would return to the island. Anguta hid himself behind some rocks near the shore.

Just as evening fell, the huge petrel arrived, walking across the water. Strands of green kelp hung from his beak. When the bird touched shore, Anguta sprang from his hiding place. He killed the petrel with one blow of his sharp bone knife.

Dizzy with relief, Sedna climbed into the kayak behind her father. Ahead of her she saw the dark line on the horizon where their village was. She was ashamed to have failed in her choice of husbands. But she was glad to be free. Anguta paddled across the waters toward home.

But the petrel had not lied to Sedna. He was indeed a prince of the sea. And the sea was angry now. The waves heard the message: the murder would have to be avenged.

Dark clouds gathered, and rain fell in torrents. The wind raged. Anguta could scarcely see. Huge waves struck the boat. They did not hit as waves usually do, one at a time. They came from all directions at once. Strong as he was, Anguta could make no progress. He paddled with all his might. But the kayak did not move any closer to shore.

Anguta was no magician. True, he had met spirits. Once he had seen spirits rise against him. He knew trails could disappear, rivers could sink, rocks could throw themselves. But such spirits were more mischievous than dangerous. Anguta knew enough to fight them off.

This was something different. This was no mischievous spirit. This was a vast force, beyond anything he had known before. The ocean itself was against him. If he continued to fight, it might turn against the whole village. It might even punish all humanity.

Anguta was a good hunter. A good hunter knows when he is outmatched. And a good hunter also knows that nature sometimes makes terrible demands. As the kayak pitched in the inky waters, Anguta paddled ferociously. From the ocean, a huge voice bellowed. It said that Sedna had caused the storm. It said that Sedna had to be returned to her husband.

But her husband was dead. The voice was demanding that Sedna, too, die. Anguta understood. If he obeyed the voice, he would lose his daughter again, but the ocean powers would be satisfied. If he refused, the ocean would kill them both—and who knew how many more humans as well.

The man turned in his kayak and grabbed his daughter's shoulders. The only kindness he knew was in not hesitating.

Sedna was frail and light. It was easy for Anguta to lift his daughter out of her seat. It was easy to throw her into the freezing water.

Sedna screamed. The water was so cold it burned. The ocean was deeper than anyone knew. She grabbed at the side of the kayak. Anguta pushed her away with his paddle. The desperate girl clung harder. Anguta hammered at Sedna's hands with his paddles. Once, twice he hit. She still clung fast. Again. Again—

Then he stopped. He put his paddle down inside the boat. He pulled his knife and cut off her fingers.

She screamed once, a piercing sound. Sedna flung her arms over the kayak's sides. But Anguta cut them off.

Sedna began to sink to the ocean. The last thing she saw was her father pushing his paddle into one of her eyes, trying to drive her sinking body farther from the boat.

The water was red from Sedna's blood. She saw dimly, from her one eye, the face of her father as she sank.

Suddenly, the water calmed, allowing Anguta to paddle home. The ocean had accepted Anguta's terrible sacrifice. But, because nature lives in balance, it gave something back for the life it had taken. For, as she sank into the freezing water, Sedna did not die. She was transformed.

The sea, empty of life before, suddenly teemed with fish of many kinds: Sedna's fingers had sprung to life. Where there had been no sea animals before, whales and seals and walrus now swam: Sedna's arms.

Flashes of silver beneath the water's surface showed where salmon were already spawning, flooding upstream so that even people far inland could feast on their red, oily flesh. Huge halibut clung to the bottom, each a hundred pounds of sweet meat. Tuna schooled through the waters, and sardines, and herring. The ocean, no longer silent, rang with the song of whales.

Never again would the Inuit have to live on roots and berries and bits of meat. Now there would be whale meat—tons of it—to mark the spring. Now there would be seal oil to light the winter home. Now there would be dried fish to live on even as the storms of winter roared around the house.

All this because of Sedna, a proud girl who had given her life so that, ever after, our lives would be richer. That life will never be easy, the Inuit know. Life brings struggle and hunger and pain, as well as love and safety. But they say "ayarnamut," which means "it cannot be otherwise."

• • •

## Goddesses of the Arctic North

In the Arctic, in the lands around the North Pole, live people who are sometimes called the Eskimo. That word, however, is actually the insulting name given to them by another nation, and means "raw fish eater." Among themselves, they are just "the people," which in their various languages may be pronounced Inuit (in Canada and Greenland), Inupiat (northern Alaska), Yup'ik (southwest Alaska), and Chuckchi (Siberia). Across thousands of miles of Arctic terrain, these people share the myth of Sedna, the great goddess who provided food from the sea. For, in the Arctic lands that Sedna's people call home, the richest source of food was the ocean, not the land. Seal, whale, walrus—these ocean mammals provided meat in plenty. And then there were the fish, especially the salmon, which teem into Arctic rivers every summer and feed bears and birds as well as people.

A rugged land needs a rugged people. The Inuit and their relatives live in perhaps the harshest land in the world. But they lack nothing that makes life meaningful. They have love, and song, and ritual, and family. They are especially fond of storytelling, which not only carries the history of their people but provides entertainment in the long winter nights. In the past, sometimes a whole village harnessed dogsleds and traveled hundreds of miles to another village, to spend a week or more exchanging stories. These included some stories of violence and pain, just as our televisions every night show shoot-'em-ups and fatal car chases as well as love and comedy. But unlike our nightly dose of blood and gore, Inuit stories included violence as a way of explaining life's mysteries.

Such a story is the great myth of Sedna. She was one of the most important Inuit goddesses, but there were others as well: the creator goddess Aakuluujjusi, who made caribou by taking off her leggings and bringing them to life; Akycha, the sun goddess who was assaulted by her brother the moon; Apasinasee, who married a dog and gave birth to the original humans; Irdlirvirisissong, the wild singer; and Kadlu, the girl who created thunder just by being a noisy little girl. Their stories were not written down but memorized and told as part of winter rituals as well as just for fun.

With the coming of modern times, the myths of the Inuit and their relatives have been written down by scholars from other cultures. At the same time, Inuit peoples have lost much of their traditional way of life. If they lived a hard life in the past, they live an equally hard—though different—life today. In Canada, many Inuit mothers today cannot nurse their children because nuclear contamination in the sea creatures that they eat passes into breast milk and poisons the children. The lessons of Sedna's myth have not been learned by all the world's people, and the Inuit are among those who suffer for that lack.

## Encountering Limitation

Like evil, limitation has haunted humanity since the beginning of culture. In our minds and hearts, we are superwomen, able to leap tall buildings at a single bound, heal all the world's hurt with a kiss, and solve the most stunningly difficult problems with our radiant minds. But in reality we stumble, we forget, we grow confused. We are not the perfect beings of our inner fantasies. We are human, with the frailties and failings of our kind.

The story of Sedna can seem, at first reading, a violent and disturbing one. The girl is, after all, killed by her own father! But if we explore the meaning of the story further, we see that there is deep wisdom in the Inuit myth. For Sedna does not die: she is transformed. And through her sacrifice, the whole world is transformed as well. Like the Christian story of Jesus, who was horribly murdered while his own mother watched, the story of Sedna is a story of salvation. But in the Inuit myth, the salvation is not to be found after death, but here on this earth, in our ordinary lives. Sedna becomes the "food dish" (the meaning of one of her names) because she suffers and dies so we all may live more comfortably.

In our own lives, too, we encounter painful situations, times when life seems too hurtful to endure. Why did Mom have to get cancer? Why did Dad have to lose his job so that we are forced to move? Why did our classmate have to be killed in an auto accident? Why does a stupid bacteria like ebola have to exist at all? Why does anyone have to die?

These questions are different than those we grappled with when we discussed the Lithuanian myth of Austrina. For the questions of why disease and death occur in the world cannot be answered in the same way as questions of why people hurt each other. Cancer is different than war. Death is not the same as rape. One is a natural process, the other a human evil. We could stop all the wars and rapes in the world, and there would still be pain and death, disease and grief.

In a Hollywood dream of youth, no one is touched by death until their middle years. And people die in an orderly sequence: grandparents first, then parents, then children. But in real life, death can change our life at any age. Even if you do not personally know someone who has passed on, you will daily hear stories about people your own age who die, sometimes horribly, from diseases and accidents that could happen in your own town, your own neighborhood.

Contemporary society has a peculiar relation to death. On the one hand, it is rarely spoken of. Those who experience a death in their family often feel that others refuse to talk about it with them—or try to hurry them past the subject. We are uncomfortable with those who have endured this experience. On the other hand, our media every night beam horrible images of death and murder into our homes as "entertainment." We pay hard-earned dollars to sit in darkened rooms to be terrified by ghoulish visions of mangled bodies, and we call it fun. There has been no society in history that has had such a confused relationship with death.

Death presents us with a serious spiritual challenge: how do we live, and live happily, in a world where someday we all will die?

This question has been asked by all spiritual traditions, all religions. There are many different answers, which shows how important the question is. Most suggest that there is some kind of life after this one, a claim that seems to be upheld by contemporary scientific research into the near-death experience. But we cannot really know what waits for us beyond that final door. We must, however, learn to live well despite that uncertainty.

# Mysteries of Womanhood and Rituals of Transformation

The myth of Sedna gives us an answer to the question of how we live in a world of death: we realize that nothing really dies, but everything is transformed into new life. Biologists sometimes say that, in nature, there is no waste, only food. Sedna, in dying, gives birth to all the sea creatures that will thereafter feed her people. We, too, when we die, give nourishment back to the earth and its creatures—all the nourishment that we took from the earth during our lives.

Birth and death are the major transformative experiences of our lives. We do not have any choice in either—neither about the timing, nor the way it will happen. We may be born prematurely or late; we may die in youth or midlife or old age. Between these enormous moments, we face other transformations as well. As women we grow, we bleed, we take lovers, we bear children, we cease to bleed. All of these are events that we experience with our bodies, and with our spirits as well.

We have some choice in these transformations—such as when, if, and with whom to have sexual relations—but we do not have complete control. Every sexual act between men and women, for instance, involves the possibility of pregnancy; even the most effective contraceptives are not 100 percent certain. Sex, too, involves the possibility of encountering disease; again, even the most effective protections sometimes fail. But does this mean we should "just say no" to all possibility of sexual relationship? No. But it does mean that those who honor the goddess take responsibility for the seriousness of such acts and think about potential consequences before acting.

In the case of the other transformations we experience—the beginning of menstruation, our monthly flow, other bodily changes, the development of a child in the womb and its birth, aging and the end of menses—we have no control of our bodies as they pass through these transformations. They are parts of the great mystery of our womanhood, a mystery that our ancestors celebrated and honored as part of the spiritual quest. Today we tend to hide these experiences, sometimes talking about them in giggles but more often keeping them secret. We do not know when our friends experience their first blood, nor the stories of our mothers when they did so. The mysteries of womanhood have become personal secrets rather than shared festivals.

On the path of the Wild Girl, you create celebrations that honor your womanhood. Our spirit expresses itself through our bodies. Every meal is a communion with the creatures who died to help us live. Every menstrual period is a reminder of the great mystery of our births and deaths. Learning to accept and embrace our physical beings is one of the most important parts of the young goddess mysteries.

# Rites of Passage

In every society, there are celebrations for the transformative moments in our lives. These are called "rites of passage," and we still celebrate some of them today. Weddings are public celebrations of the joining of two lives that may lead to new life. Funerals celebrate the life of the deceased as well as the mystery of death. But there are many other moments in our lives that we can mark with ceremonies. Here are some suggestions.

### First Blood Ceremony
For a girl who has begun to menstruate, a ceremony is traditional in most cultures. Often this involves having women, including the girl's mother, welcome her to the circle of womanhood. This can also be done with friends who have had their first periods serving as the welcomers. Rituals should include some farewell to childhood, perhaps through changing clothing or hairstyle. Emblems such as red roses are appropriate gifts. The girl receiving the honors at such a ceremony should meditate upon her own vision of what a powerful and successful woman she will be. You can celebrate your first blood and your initiation into womanhood at any time. If you were not welcomed into the circle of womanhood with your first period, choose another time for that celebration (see chapter 11 for ideas).

### Monthly Blood Ceremony
After the ritual of first blood, women can ritualize their monthly blood as well. Even a simple ritual like wearing a necklace with a red stone or lighting a red candle can be sufficient, so long as the intention of honoring women's mysteries is held in the mind. Remember that ritual combines action and

intention (see chapter 2). Create a ritual that reminds you of the power of women throughout time.

### Sexual Initiation Ceremony

For many women, sexual initiation is awkward, painful, even dangerous. This should not be the case. Sexual activity should be chosen freely and carefully. A partner who loves you and whom you love, a safe setting, and concern for contraception and disease prevention are primary. If you are considering undergoing a sexual initiation, create for yourself a series of ceremonies in which you prepare yourself for the love you deserve, through meditation and ritual blessings. Then ask your partner in initiation to engage in self-blessing or similar activity before you offer yourself to sexual activity. A partner who mocks your desire to celebrate your womanhood in this way is unworthy of you. Even more importantly, a partner who refuses to protect you from the possibility of sexually transmitted disease and/or pregnancy is not only unworthy but dangerous. It would be better to wait for another partner who will make your sexual initiation a memorable and spiritual experience. If you do not have that opportunity to share an initiation ritual with your lover, try to take time afterward to honor yourself and your body's power. Similarly, if you never had a sexual initiation ceremony when you first engaged in sexual activity, you can create one for yourself at any time.

### Sexual Joy Rituals

Like the monthly blood ceremonies that continue the work you began with your first blood ceremony, you can continue to honor your womanly beauty and power by creating rituals each time you engage in sexual activity. Remember that ritual involves intention and action. You need not create a lot of hocus pocus around yourself to act upon your intention that every sexual activity be joy-producing. You might consider a tattoo of a meaningful symbol in a place where only a lover can see it. Or you may put on a special perfume when you are about to make love, blessing yourself as you do so. A candle can be lit in conscious reverence. Remember that anyone who cannot accept your spiritual self is not a good partner to you. If you remain with such a person, your life will not have room for the true lover who can partner the Wild Girl within you.

## Activities for Mysterious Wild Girls

 Create a self-blessing ritual. Write a short statement of your strength and beauty and intelligence, or locate one that you find appropriate. Using an oil or ointment or incense, speak aloud the words while touching yourself. Bless your feet and legs for carrying you through the world, your pelvis for cradling your central organs, your belly for its potential, your breasts for their nourishing power, your hands for doing your important work, your mouth for speaking your truth, your eyes for seeing opportunity. Use this blessing with all your rites of transformation, and whenever you feel you have forgotten your own power and strength.

 Talk to your female relatives. Find out from your mother and your grandmother, and your great-grandmother if she still lives, what their experiences of womanhood have been. Ask your aunts and sisters and cousins about their experiences. Talk with them about your emerging sense of your womanly power. They may feel ill at ease at first, because this is not common in our culture. But persist. There is someone among your relatives who will be your link to the womanly history of your family.

 Read about other cultures and their understanding of womanhood. In doing so, look especially for works by woman authors, who may be especially sensitive to the problems and opportunities women face. Read fantasy and science fiction, too, which offer models of how women can be both strong and attractive. Use the ideas and images from these works in creating your Wild Girl rituals.

Go to a museum to look for goddess images. Do not start by looking at the labels; look at the pictures and sculptures instead. Look for images that feel powerful and womanly to you. Photograph or copy them if you can, or buy a card or other reproduction of the images for your altar or your purse. If you do not live near a museum (or even if you do!), go to the library and look through books of ancient and tribal art, enjoying the goddess images. Make color photocopies of your favorites for your diary or altar.

 Make a heroine collage. Create an image for your wall or your altar by collecting photographs of women who embody, for you, the power and beauty of womanhood. Do not hurry; it may take several months to collect enough images. Be sure to include images of woman at all ages, so you can imagine yourself as powerful and beautiful when you are older as well as when you are young. Gather images as well of natural beauties that seem to you to be feminine and lovely: waterfalls, mountains, flowers. Cut up magazines and photocopy images from books. When you feel you have enough (perhaps forty images), create a collage with them. Cut the women's images from their backgrounds and arrange them on a light cardboard backing in a pleasing pattern (you might want to put them in a circle or other significant symbol) and glue them down. Sprinkle images of nature in among the women, so that your inner eye can see the connection between nature's beauty and the beauty of womanhood.

. . .

## 9

# *Beyond the Turtle Ocean, Above the Western Sky*

## Korea

**B**yul-Soon woke up sick, her eyes swollen almost shut. Her throat ached and itched. It had been days since she had been able to struggle out of bed. For days she had been tossing and turning, sleeping heavily, dreaming fiery dreams.

"Enough," her mother said that morning. "I will call the doctor." She felt the girl's forehead again, nodding sharply. "This has gone on too long."

A few doors away lived Kim Soon-Ham, a doctor who used the old ways of healing. Her mother had treated Byul-Soon's mother. Even their grandmothers had been friends. Kim Soon-Ham herself had been a doctor for more than twenty years, since her mother had retired.

It took a few hours for arrangements to be made. By afternoon Kim Soon-Ham arrived with Han Yoon, her assistant, carrying the necessary materials. She had candles, beautiful many-colored fruits, painted fans, and a round drum, its leather skin painted on both sides.

Clearing a small space in the middle of the room, Kim Soon-Ham lit candles. Over her jeans and shirt, she pulled on a lemon-colored silk overdress with a high bodice—traditional Korean attire. Han Yoon sat down at the foot of the bed and began to drum softly. The rhythm was tentative at first, but grew stronger as the moments passed. Kim Soon-Ham stood in the center of the room, her eyes closed, concentrating intently. She stood on her toes and stretched upward. Then she began to dance.

At first her dance was simple. Over and over, she bounced on her heels and into the air. The drummer drummed and the candles flickered. Kim Soon-Ham danced this way for almost an hour. Then, grabbing the short sword she wore by her side, she danced around the room, cutting at the air, and cutting evil influences away from the sick girl.

The doctor did not rest for hours. She danced and danced in the close heat of the sickroom. All the time her face was intent, her eyes black and distant. No one knew what she saw when she disappeared behind her eyes like that. It was said that she visited other worlds, looking for the cause of sickness.

All of a sudden the doctor stopped dancing. Her assistant stopped drumming. The silence boomed. It was broken when the doctor began to tell a story. In the silence of the sickroom, she recited the following story.

It was many, many years ago that a girl named Pali Kongju lived on Earth, in the kingdom of Sam. She was the youngest daughter of King Upbi and Queen Guide. Years earlier, when they had met and fallen in love, a fortuneteller told them not to marry right away, or bad luck would fall upon the family. The following year, the fortuneteller said, would be a good one in which to marry.

"Nonsense!" said the king. He was in love, and he did not wish to wait a year. The wedding was held the next week.

A few months later, the excited people learned that their new queen was bearing a child. A daughter was born. The next year, another daughter was born. The next year, another. Year after year, the queen gave birth to daughters.

The queen loved her beautiful children, but the king wanted a son. He believed that his subjects would not respect him if he did not have a prince in the palace.

In the seventh year, the queen became pregnant again. In her dreams, she saw two dragons, one blue and one yellow. They coiled around a high pillar from which heavenly music flowed. Clouds of all colors swirled around the dragons. It was a beautiful, mysterious dream.

"That dream," the king announced, "is an omen. It means you will give birth to my prince."

The queen said nothing. She did not know what the dream meant, but she feared her husband's disappointment at another daughter. When the queen's labor began, she secluded herself and refused to see the king.

When the first sharp cry of the new baby sounded in the palace halls, the king came running. "Is it my prince?" he asked a servant.

The servant, wisely, said nothing at all.

He grabbed another servant, who also said nothing. Growing more furious, he found the queen's personal maid and pulled her hair until she said that, yes, the child was born. And no, it was not a prince.

The king blew up like a volcano. "I will not have another daughter!" he yelled. "Throw that child away! Take it to the ocean and drown it! Make sure I never, ever see that child!"

The servants pulled away in fear. One of them, more tender-hearted than the others, managed a question.

"Would you throw the child away without even giving it a name?" she murmured.

"I'll give her a name," the king fumed. "Call her Pali Kongju!"

The servants wept. The name meant "Princess Thrown-Away."

Not even the queen could convince the king to change his mind. So a weeping Queen Guide put Pali Kongju in a little box with jewels on the outside. She gave the baby a bottle of milk on which to nurse and wrote a little note saying, "This child is a princess. Please be very kind to her."

And with that, the box was taken by the king's guard and dropped into the sea from a high cliff. It fell into the water with a big splash. The soldiers stood for a moment to watch the box, and the baby, sink below the waves.

Instead, they saw something wonderful. Hundreds of turtles, all golden, rose from the bottom of the sea. They swam together, forming a golden raft on which the little box floated, safe and dry.

The box floated across the ocean to a shore far away from the raging king. There the turtles placed it on the beach. And there it was found, not long after, by Piri and Kongdok. They were old and poor, but they were the kindest people in the world. When they saw the baby inside the jeweled box, their hearts warmed. Immediately they brought the tiny princess home.

Somehow, from then on, there was enough to eat. Not a single kernel of rice fell unripe in the bright-green paddy. Not a single head of cabbage wilted before it could be preserved. Somehow there was enough wood to heat the tiny house each winter. Life was not rich for Piri and Kongdok, but it was no longer poor.

And every day they enjoyed the richness of their love for Pali Kongju. She was a bright child who asked many questions. When she was about eight, she began to ask who she really was, for she knew she could not be the child of such old people. They told her she came from the ocean on the backs of golden turtles. She shook her head and pursed her lips. She knew that was impossible. But Piri and Kongdok stuck by their story.

A few more years passed. Back in the kingdom of Sam, King Upbi and Queen Guide had become very sick. Famous doctors came from around the world to try to cure them. But no matter what treatment they used or what medicines they administered, the royal couple grew worse.

In despair, the king called for the fortuneteller who had warned them against marrying.

"There is a way to cure your illness," said the fortuneteller.

"Good," moaned the king, "tell us. Tell us now."

"It will be very hard."

"I do not care," said the king. "Tell us."

"Only one thing can cure you: water from a well in the Western Sky."

"But," the king cried, pulling himself up on one elbow, "no one can go there! It is beyond heaven itself!"

"Yes," said the fortuneteller, "but one person can go there."

"Tell us!" the king demanded in his weak, hoarse voice.

"Your seventh daughter," said the fortuneteller.

The king and queen looked at each other silently. Tears filled the queen's eyes. "Then we will die," she said. "You killed that child." And all the years of pain ran down her cheeks.

"Oh, no," said the fortuneteller, who could see both the past and the future. "She still lives."

"She lives!" the queen cried. "Where?"

"That I will not tell you. You must search for her yourself."

The fortuneteller left the palace then, rewarded with riches for her information. But the king and queen were still dreadfully sick. The search for the healing water had to begin soon.

The king still could not believe that Princess Thrown-Away was still alive and would save him. Before searching for her, he called his other daughters to him.

To the oldest he said, "We are dying. We must have the heavenly water from the Western Kingdom."

"But generals and warriors do not dare go there! How could I?"

He turned to the next. "Save us," he said. "Go to the Western Kingdom."

"But I'm just a helpless woman," she said. "I do not dare."

He turned to the third and made the same plea.

"But I do not even go outside," she said, shuddering. "I hate going outside. And I do not know east from west."

The fourth was next in line.

"How can I dare go where my older sisters do not dare?"

And the fifth, and the sixth, said exactly the same words.

The king would have been furious, but he was growing weaker by the moment. The last chance was Pali Kongju, the rejected princess. But where was she?

At that moment, she was outside her home, playing in the woods. Pali Kongju was a girl whose special talent was understanding birds and animals. Often she went into the forest. There she spent the days watching birds flutter by, seeing an occasional deer paw at the underbrush, laughing as squirrels chattered in the treetops.

It was there she was when suddenly the wind spoke to her. "Princess," the wind said, "go home immediately. Your parents are dying."

Stricken with fear, Pali Kongju ran home. But there were her foster parents, working in their tiny garden, hoeing the cabbages.

"I thought you were dying!" she said, throwing herself into her mother's arms.

When she told them what had happened, the old man and old woman looked at each other. It was time to tell the princess who she really was.

From the toolshed they brought the jeweled box and the note Pali Kongju had carried with her on her ocean voyage. They gave her directions to the palace and, weeping, they bid her farewell.

At the palace, the girl gazed with wonder at the upswept roof that looked like a lady picking up her skirts, at the multicolored designs that covered every wall, at the bright silks everyone wore. There she stood, a peasant girl in a handmade smock, until someone noticed her.

"I am Princess Thrown-Away," she said simply.

Her words caused a commotion. Servants began to run everywhere. It was only moments before word reached the room where the king and queen lay dying. Weeping with delight, they sent for the visitor to come to their bedside.

The moment they saw her, they knew she was their daughter. She had her father's strong forehead, her mother's dimpled chin. When she gave them the note proving her identity, it confirmed what they already knew.

"Oh, seventh princess, you must save us!" said the king. Forgetting that he had thrown this daughter into the ocean, he demanded that she travel to the Western Sky to save him.

Pali Kongju did not resist. "A child's duty is to save her parents," she said. She asked for iron shoes and an iron stick for her journey. When they were brought to her, she set off.

The Kingdom of the Western Sky is a secret place, one to which no directions exist. There was no map for her to follow. No visitors had ever returned from that place. There was no one to ask for help. But Princess Pali started down the road leading west, trusting that she would find her way.

A day's walk from the palace, the land grew hilly. The next day Pali Kongju climbed the sides of steep mountains. She climbed beyond all roads, hoping that she was headed in the right direction. The mountains grew steeper and steeper. Some of them had caps of snow at their head. On top of one of these she discovered two mountain gods playing a game of cards.

"Excuse me," said the princess politely. "Do you know the way to the kingdom of the Western Sky?"

There was no reply. The gods concentrated on their game.

For days they played. Pali Kongju, not knowing what else to do, sat and watched them.

At last, however, the game ended. When it did, the gods flew right up into the sky.

Pali Kongju cried out in dismay. Noticing her for the first time, the gods returned to Earth. The girl bowed to them and asked them politely for directions to the Western Sky.

"You! A girl! You cannot make such a journey!" said one god.

"Not even warriors have returned!" said the other.

"But my parents will die without the water from the magical well there. I must go."

The gods withdrew to the sky for a few moments to discuss the problem. Convinced that the girl would go on with or without their help, they decided to lend their aid.

"I cannot myself tell you the Secret of Heaven," said one god. "But I know someone who will. Ask the old woman who is plough-ing up the mountain right next door."

Then they disappeared up into the sky. Pali Kongju walked down the mountain path and up the next mountain. There, as she had been told, she found an old woman. Though she had deep lines in her face, the woman was very strong: she was ploughing a field with her bare hands. "Grandmother," said Princess Pali politely, "can you tell me the way to the Western Sky?"

"What can you pay for it?" snarled the old woman.

"I have no money with me," said Pali Kongju, "because I left in a hurry. But I am willing to work for you."

The old woman's eyes lit up. "Well," she said, "then plow this field."

The field was huge. It was filled with rocks and stinging nettles. There were stumps of trees everywhere. And there was no plow.

Undeterred, Pali Kongju set to work plowing the field with her bare hands. She worked and worked. Finally the rocky field was cleared. But then the old woman demand she plant the field. And then she demanded that she tend the growing plants. Finally, the old woman demanded the princess harvest the crop.

At last, when all the work was done, the old woman said to Pali Kongju, "It's easy. Go straight across the mountain. When you find an old woman washing clothes, ask her. She knows."

So Pali Kongju set off again, climbing one mountain and then the next. Finally she came to a woman washing clothes in a clear mountain stream.

"Lady," said the princess politely, "may I inquire the way to the Western Sky?"

"I will tell you," the woman said, "but only if you wash these clothes white." And she threw her a bundle of black laundry.

Pali Kongju set to work scrubbing the black clothes in the cold mountain stream. Her hands chafed and hurt from the effort, but after days of work, she had turned the clothing white.

"I respect your faith and your effort," said the magical lady. "This stream is the path to the Western Sky."

So Pali Kongju walked along the banks of the stream. She followed it as it widened into a river and then flowed into the ocean. The sea opened out before her, with no path visible.

As she stood there, wondering what to do next, she saw the water move as though it were boiling. From the water came golden turtles, hundreds of them, swimming fast. They came together in the sea and formed an arched golden bridge. On it, Pali Kongju walked across the ocean. On the other side, she found a forest of thorn bushes through which she had to push her way. Within it, she found a deep well of cold water. And there, next to the well, she found a spirit woman, weeping.

"I was sent here to get water," she sobbed, "but I have broken my water jar." It lay next to her, shattered. Pali Kongju set to work assembling the pieces and sticking them together with sap from the surrounding thorn trees. At last the spirit-woman's jar was fixed. She stopped weeping and smiled at Pali Kongju.

"What can I do to repay you?" she asked.

"Tell me the way to the Well at the Western Sky," Pali Kongju said.

"Of course. It's right over there," the woman said. Then she pointed to a green valley several mountains away.

Pali Kongju started climbing again and, in a few days, had reached the green valley. But there an ugly giant stood guard. "What are you doing here?" he sneered at the girl.

"I am the seventh princess from the kingdom of Sam," said Pali Kongju proudly, "and I have come to fetch healing water for my parents."

"And do you have any way to pay for this healing water?" the giant demanded.

"No," said Pali Kongju. "I was in a hurry when I left, and I didn't know the water would cost anything."

"You didn't know!" said the giant. "But you still need to pay! So you can marry me!"

Pali Kongju was on a mountaintop at the edge of the world. There was no way she would ever get back without help. Within her, something told the princess that this was the right thing to do. So she married the giant and settled down to make a home for him.

She bore seven sons, all beautiful young men. Time passes differently in the heavenly world than on Earth. A few hours here can be a lifetime there, or a lifetime here passes in a blink there. The princess married and had sons and the sons grew up, all in a few Earth hours.

But they were the very hours the King and Queen died. Suddenly, a god appeared on Pali's mountaintop with a flower boat to sail her home. Calling to her sons to accompany her, she dipped a pitcher of water from the Western Sky's well and climbed into the boat.

It took much less time to return than it had to ascend to the Western Sky. Princess Pali arrived just in time for her parents' funeral. Running toward the coffins that contained their withered bodies, Pali Kongju threw the Western Sky's water over them.

A shudder went through each of the corpses. Then their eyes opened. As the king and queen looked up, they saw their seventh daughter looking down at them.

"Pali Kongju," they cried out together. "You have saved us!" The king and queen sat up in their coffins and embraced their lost daughter.

All around them, the palace attendants were celebrating. In a corner, the six sisters gathered, glaring at their sister, Pali Kongju, in anger. They had almost been queens of the entire land, but now they were merely princesses again.

"I will give you my entire treasure," said the king. "Only you have been a good daughter."

But Pali Kongju did not forget that this king had thrown her into the ocean when she was born. This king had named her "Princess Thrown-Away." She owed him the respect of a daughter, but nothing more.

Pali Kongju had done her duty. She had proven her strength in doing so. Now she wanted to go home.

"I need no treasures," she said quietly. "I have done what I set out to do. I have shown that I can travel to the heavenly kingdoms and return. No warrior could do that. No general ever did what I, a rejected daughter, have done. Now I will go home."

With that, she walked away from the palace toward the west, to rejoin her giant husband in their land.

And that was the end of the story, the tale of the world's first doctor. It is still told today in Korea, like a prayer when someone is sick. It is told by doctors such as the one who stood in Byul-Soon's bedroom. Her words hung in the air. Somberly, the dancing doctor bent over Byul-Soon and looked deeply into her eyes.

"Whenever a person dies," she said to the girl, "and cannot find her way to peace, we tell the story of Pali Kongju. You have been sick because a spirit wandered through this house and found you. She did not know that she was dead, so she sat in your body trying to speak. That is why your throat hurt. It was her pain. Now, she is gone. She has gone to her afterlife. You will be well now."

The assistant blew out the candles and packed them away. Byul-Soon's mother saw the two women to the door, murmuring her thanks and slipping some money into the doctor's pocket.

In her bedroom, Byul-Soon cried a little, thinking of the dead lady who had sat in her body for several weeks. Then, sighing, she slipped into a deep, healing sleep.

• • •

## Goddesses of Korea

In Korea, the narrow peninsula that points from China toward Japan, a women's religion has been practiced for more than two thousand years. It is the religion of the *mudang*, the dancing doctors who heal both body and spirit. This religion tells us that there are many levels to the world—both seen and unseen, upper and lower—connected by an invisible ladder or rope. A shaman is one who can travel between these upper and lower worlds on that invisible ladder, bringing healing as they do so.

This shamanic religion still exists today. While in some lands, shamans are men, in Korea they are almost all women. As many as 100,000 shamans live in Korea today, dancing their ritual healings for members of their community. They consider themselves the spiritual descendents of Pali Kongju, the first woman to have ever conquered the spirit realm to offer healing on Earth. The story of how, despite being thrown away by her parents, she braved unknown ghostly lands is told as part of the *kut* or dance ritual of the mudang.

In the kut, the woman shaman tries to discover the reasons for illness and unhappiness. She begins with the simple bouncing dance that the shaman uses to gain a trancelike state so that she may enter the other worlds. Once she has become entranced, she learns the information that her client needs. These kuts are held every day in Korea and in Korean communities throughout the world. Whenever and wherever they are held, the heritage of the girl savior, the world's first doctor, is celebrated.

## Dancing Your Own Dance

Today we think of dance as a form of entertainment, but throughout history, dance has been a spiritual experience. Simple circle dances are still danced in American Indian pow-wows today, part of an unbroken tradition of spiritual movement on this continent. Some Asian meditations, like tai chi, rely upon slow, repetitive motions to encourage serenity and spiritual awareness. Many European folk-dances were originally ritual movements designed to encourage the growth of plants, the steady motion of the planets, the passage of the seasons.

Like the ladder that the shaman uses to move between the upper and lower worlds, dance joins body, mind, and spirit. Our body moves when we are dancing—that is, of course, the definition of dance—but our spirits soar as well. Try dancing when you are feeling depressed. Either you will stop dancing, or your mood will change (possibly growing worse before it grows better). We may become emotionally exhilarated as we dance, or we may suddenly weep. Dancing, whether by oneself or with others, whether fast or slow, whether to music or to the music of our beating hearts, is one of humanity's primary religious experiences.

In Korea, the dance is used deliberately as a means of moving beyond this world and into the next. Shamans perform repetitive dances each time they wish to assist a healing. But other women dance as part of kut rituals as well. Their dance, called the *mugam*, is individual to each woman. It is a dance that arises from her deepest soul and expresses her true individuality.

We, too, dance our own dance, even when we are unaware of it. Human beings are as unlike as snowflakes, which we praise for their uniqueness. We, too, are entirely unlike anyone who has ever lived before or will ever live again.

Learning to appreciate our unique beauties is part of every woman's personal quest. When the women of Korea dance their own dances, one might be slow and another fast, one rhythmic and another freeform. Yet all are beautiful, because all rise from the heart. Many of us, however, are not dancing our mugam. We are trying to look like and act like everyone else—afraid or ashamed of our uniqueness.

The human need to be accepted by others is very strong, strong enough to overpower our need to be seen for our uniqueness. We fear that, if we are unlike others, we will not be loved and appreciated. And anyone who has seen girls insulted and humiliated for being different—for dressing different, for talking different, for being smarter or less smart than others, for being taller or shorter or fatter—knows that there is good reason for that fear.

One of the most challenging aspects of the Wild Girl path is to learn to appreciate self and others, to accept people as they are and ourselves as we are. This is not to say that change is impossible or that improvement should not be sought. But why try to make a giraffe into a panther? There are some things about each of us that are basic, essential to our individuality, unchangeable. Wisdom rests in learning what is uniquely ours, and in embracing and accepting that.

Wisdom also means learning to accept others for what they are. This does not mean we need to accept bad behavior from others—behavior that makes us suffer. But it does mean that a Wild Girl must be wary of mocking other girls for things they cannot change. This often happens when groups are together. We have all been with groups when someone is held up to ridicule. Everyone begins to compete to be more insulting toward that absent person. Shrill laughter and nasty facial expressions show how much we disdain the person we are discussing.

We also know how poisoned we feel after such an experience. It is like eating something rotten. Yet the next time we are tempted to make fun of another girl, we join right in. And we live in dread that somewhere, someone is saying things like that about us.

Why do we do this? Because we want to be part of a group of friends, and one way of bonding together is to exclude others. It becomes a kind of bullying, with everyone afraid of each others' comments. And it results in girls, and women, being afraid to be different, to be strange, to be unique. Oh, you might dress differently than the girls you reject, but your group can be picked out by your clothing and jewelry and posture and activities.

There is nothing wrong with being part of a group, but when a group spends more of its time talking about other girls than on its own activities, things are out of balance. It becomes a kind of emotional terrorism: you feel held hostage because to leave the group would subject you to the awful talk that has been aimed at others. If you examine such a group's history, you will find that it has turned on its own members in the past. You are not safe, in such a group, from the destructive effects of gossip, whether you leave or stay. It is better to leave and find better friends who have something more to do than talk about others.

At the same time, part of the Wild Girl path is to find the strength to be yourself despite what others might say about you. Your spiritual interests may seem odd to others. Your family may not have as much money as others. You may not care to engage in some activities. You may want to pursue some activities that others judge as strange. If you let what others say about you determine your life, you will never be happy, because you will lead someone else's life, not your own. There are always people who will say hurtful things because of their own fears. The best innoculation against such bullies is to realize that, even if you changed, they would still not like you. They would find something else to complain about, to use to humiliate you. Get away from such people, stay away, and do not listen to what they say.

Share the space you create for yourself only with others who agree to support you in your spiritual quest. You may have to endure some times of solitude as you engage in that quest—not because there is anything wrong with you, but because being alone is part of the quest. In the secret space you make when you separate yourself from negative companions, you can let your own music play and you can dance your own dance. In doing so, you will find your way to others who dance the way you do.

## Making a Spiritual Diary

One way to find your own truth is to keep a spiritual diary. This is different from a regular diary in which you write things that happen in your outer world: where you went, who you saw, what you ate. A spiritual diary focuses on your inner life and includes only details of your quest.

There is no one true way to keep a spiritual diary. You can do it by handwriting or typing. You can use spiral binders, blank papers, or even handmade papers. You can write with colored pen or ballpoint. You can illustrate the diary with sketches and drawings, cut out pictures for illustrations, or have no illustrations at all. You can have several, even many, spiritual diaries, or you can put everything in one book. You can combine your spiritual diary with your dream diary (chapter 4) or keep them separate.

Whatever way you decide to keep your spiritual diary, you need to follow only two rules: do not share it with anyone, and be consistent in your use of it.

The first rule is important because you need space and privacy to develop a spiritual practice. If you post your spiritual diary every day on your homepage, you will never experience the secret spaces of your soul that cry out to be explored. We all need a place to be silly as well as serene, to be weepy as well as wise. We need a place to take off our masks. Your spiritual diary allows you such freedom. Sharing it with others, even with your Wild Girl friends, denies you that secret exploration.

Sometimes you may be tempted to read a passage or to show a picture from your diary to another. Ask yourself why you are doing this. Most often, it is because we want approval from that person. But why let another person stand as judge over your spiritual life? If they approve, you will try to do the same thing again, even if it was not really good for you. If they disapprove, you will stop—even if what you wrote was profoundly important to you. Sharing your spiritual diary diffuses its power.

But there are also occasions where someone reads your diary without your permission. This is an invasion of privacy, even if the person makes a joke about it or claims they had the right. It is not funny, and they did not have the right. From the start, find a safe place to keep your journal. If you suspect someone has been reading it, move it to another safe place.

Some people, like the great artist Beatrix Potter of Peter Rabbit fame, kept their diaries in code so that no one could spy on them. If you are afraid that you will not have the privacy you need, you can keep various kinds of spiritual diaries, like the commonplace book and the sketch diary (see page 148), which are hard to interpret and so provide their own cloaking devices.

In addition to privacy, consistency is important. Like any spiritual practice, your spiritual diary becomes more powerful the more you use it. Set aside some regular time in your sacred space for writing in your spiritual diary. You need not write every day. You may choose, for instance, to write only on significant days, such as solstices and other festivals. The point of a spiritual diary is not to record everything that has ever happened to you. Rather, it serves two purposes. Obviously, it documents your path so that you can later remember it. But it is also part of the exploration itself. The process of expressing your spiritual realities brings them more clearly into focus. Recording in your diary is a kind of meditation.

# Ideas for Your Spiritual Diary

There are many ways to keep a spiritual diary. Here are some, which can be combined in one volume or kept in separate volumes. Another form of diary is the dream dictionary described in chapter 4.

### The Commonplace Book

This is an old form of diary-keeping that involves copying significant passages from books and other sources, such as movies and conversations. It is nice to keep a commonplace collection in a fancy, hand-bound book. It can go on for many years, and you can trace your spiritual evolution by re-reading what spoke to you at different times. You may wish to date the entries.

### The Book of Shadows

This is a traditional kind of spiritual diary in which rituals and ceremonies are written. Often kept in a special volume, which may be decorated both outside and inside, the Book of Shadows is a place to write the prayers you speak and actions you take in your ritual work. You may copy material from other sources or write down notes from spiritual leaders in your Book of Shadows, thus creating another kind of commonplace book, or the rituals may all be composed by you.

### The Sketch Diary

You do not have to be an artist to keep a spiritual sketch diary. You only need to set time aside to draw out the images from your dreams, meditations, and other spiritual moments. The medium does not matter: use pencil, pen, colored inks, watercolors, collage. You may wish to write poetic descriptions of the images you create.

### The Daily Diary

Like the traditional daily diary in which you write the events of your life, this kind of diary requires you to spend some time every day writing. However, instead of focussing on the outer world, in this diary you focus on the inner one. What did you think today? What challenges did you face? How did you meet them?

### Thought Diary

In French, this is called a *pensées* diary and has been used by many great thinkers, like Blaise Pascal and Simone Weil. In this diary, you limit yourself to one sentence every day. Into that sentence, you must condense all the spiritual knowledge you have gained that day.

### Poetry Diary

Like the thought diary, this should be kept every day as a meditation. You may wish to use a simple poetic form, like haiku, or you may prefer writing in free verse. Write one poem every day, on events and ideas from that day. You may wish to use such a diary to find ideas for later development into finished poems, but that is not necessary.

### Vision Diary

If you are interested in shamanic work or other spiritual exercises that take you into dreamlike or trace states, a diary in which you record your visions is very useful. You may wish to illustrate it as well as write descriptions of your journeys.

### Nature Diary

Because part of your life as a Wild Girl is to get to know the plants and wildlife of your area, keeping a nature diary can help you remember what you have learned. Press leaves of plants, do sketches of birds, and record dramatic weather in such a diary.

## Activities for Spiritual Wild Girls

 Learn about herbs. Herbs are one of the primary forms of healing in traditional medicines. Do you know that the same chemical found in aspirin is found naturally in willow bark? Do you know that you can heal burns with aloe? Especially if you are in the habit of taking many over-the-counter remedies, learn about herbal substitutes. Use the real herbs, brewed into tisanes (herbal teas), rather than capsules.

 Make a new friend. Reach out to someone different from you: someone of a different age, race, or religion, someone from a different neighborhood or country. You can do this in person or through the Internet. Ask that person about their spiritual life and listen with attention.

 If you or a friend are in physical or emotional pain, hold a healing circle. If the sufferer can be there, place her in the center of the circle; otherwise hold an image of her in your minds. Sit in a circle and hold hands. Imagine white light surrounding the person and healing her. Hold this meditation for at least a half-hour.

 Take a magical walk. Walk alone, slowly, through a natural place—a woodland or a park, a beach or a lakeside. As you do so, pay attention to the living things that surround you. Look carefully as well at the rocks and soil. Something will take your eye, offering it to you as though it is a gift. It is a gift from the universe to you. Before taking it, stand awhile in meditation and silently ask the place if it does, indeed, wish to give you the gift. When you are certain the answer is yes, accept the gift thankfully. Put it on your altar or in your sacred pouch (page 151).

Make a sacred pouch. Sometimes called a medicine bag, this is a small bag you can wear around your neck to hold spiritual objects. To make one, cut a circle between 4–6 inches in diameter of felt (you can also use cloth if you hem the edges). Decorate one side, using fabric paints or yarn, in designs that have spiritual significance to you (spirals, circles, and other symbolic shapes make good decorations). Then, using a large needle and a 24-inch piece of doubled yarn, sew in simple running stitches a circle 1½ inches in from the edge. Leave a 10-inch tail of yarn at the beginning and, when you have reached the end, draw the thread together so that it gathers the material. Tie loosely; you will want to be able to open and close your pouch to add additional objects. Once an object has been placed in the pouch, do not take it out; let its power remain secret and protected.

- - -

# 10

# *An Old Song, Bravely Sung*

## Africa

Sabulana lived in a village on the edge of the African forest. She was a lively young woman, full of questions, eager to learn. Her dark eyes shone in her brown face, curious and intelligent. Sabulana was the kind of girl who, everyone agreed, would grow up to lead her people.

But Sabulana did not have to wait to grow up.

Sabulana lived where food was plentiful. No one ever went hungry, for the village gardens grew huge crops of okra and peanuts, beans and yams. The forest and plains were full of game, from the tiny gazelle to the massive elephant, so there was always meat in the stew Sabulana's mother served. And there was wild honey and fruit from the forests for dessert. Life was good.

When Sabulana was a little girl, her people practiced the old ways. They left a corner of the field unplowed in honor of the goddess of the soil. In her honor, they never worked on Thursdays, resting with the earth. They respected all living creatures, especially pregnant animals. And they saw all women as images of the goddess. In return, they believed that the goddess gave them food.

But as years passed, people stopped practicing the old ways. Some derided them as superstition: why obey those silly old rules? Others were just lazy: why obey old rules when life was easier without them? Still others were greedy: why leave those corners unplowed when more crops could be planted there?

Slowly, Sabulana's people forgot the rules of the goddess. And slowly, food became less plentiful. One year the bean crop failed. But we can live without beans, the people said. And so they did. But the next year the peanut crop failed. Then it was yams that failed. Each year, food grew more scarce. The trees stopped bearing fruit, the bees stopped hoarding honey in their hives, wild game was no longer seen around the village.

Years passed. Farmers still plowed each spring, but barely a sprout came up. Weeds invaded the gardens and grew so fast they towered over even the tallest man. Women put their hands into old tree stumps, trying to find honey, and pulled them out screaming, their hands bleeding from the stings of starving bees.

People began to die. No one could figure out why food was so scarce. Had there not always been food? Their leaders invented magical ceremonies, but none of them worked. It occurred to no one to connect the lost old ways with the shortage of food.

People squatted miserably before their houses, moaning for hours at a time. Little children sat and stared, their swollen bellies full of air. The people grew so weak that they could not even look for food. Hopelessness set in throughout the village. The few beans left over from planting were devoured. People even ate their leather shoes and capes. They drank dirty water every few hours, hoping the dirt would make the empty feeling in their stomachs go away.

Sabulana felt the pain as much as any of them. But she was not hopeless: optimistic and determined by nature, she believed that something could be done. She began thinking carefully. "Let me see," she thought. "I was five when the gardens started failing. What was life like before that? Were we doing something differently?"

While everyone else sat and stared at the ground, wishing the hunger would stop, Sabulana pondered. As she considered the problem, she remembered a place in the forest called the grove of the ancestors. No one went there any more, because they were afraid of ghosts. But the ancestors—they would certainly know how things were done in the old days!

In the old days, things had been better. There had been food in plenty. So Sabulana pulled herself to her feet. Slowly and painfully, supporting herself on a stick she'd fashioned into a crutch, she moved toward the grove. The other children watched her. Small and bony now, with protruding cheekbones and eyes, they stared at the girl.

"Where are you going, Sabulana?" one whispered.

"I am going to the grove of the ancestors."

The other children pulled back in fear. "The grove? Do not go there! There are ghosts!"

"What do I care? " Sabulana said. "I am starving. What could a ghost do that would be worse?"

Slowly, painfully, she walked toward the grove. As she reached it, she felt a chill of fear. She'd heard tales about this grove, how people sometimes disappeared into it. But she would soon be dead anyway, she told herself. And everyone else would be dead with her, if she did not find out what the ancestors knew.

The grove, dark with the shade of old trees, was cooler than the plain where the village stood. Sabulana dragged herself over gnarled roots, unsure of where she was going. The cold was unfamiliar to her, whose skin felt the burning sun all day. At the center of the grove she found an open spot. There she sat down, holding her walking stick in front of her like a weapon. There she waited.

Suddenly there was a rush of wind.

She felt the ancestors even before she saw them. Slowly they emerged, big-headed and long-legged, looking more like statues than like people. They stood around her like a dark forest. They began to hoot and cackle at her. The noise was deafening.

"Ancestors, I am Sabulana," she called, over the din. They waved their bony arms and moved toward her threateningly.

Sabulana was not sure what they could do to her. Nor did she know how to defend herself. As they grew closer and closer, screaming at her, she suddenly decided what to do.

She began to sing. They were screaming like babies, so she sang them a lullaby. She sang in a thin piping voice, full of fear and hunger. She kept singing, verse after verse.

The ancestors formed a ring around Sabulana. They stared at her and pointed. Then one began to cry. Another sniffled. The girl sang the lullaby all the way to the end. Then there was silence in the grove.

Finally, an ancestor woman spoke. "That lullaby. I sang it to my baby, who died when he was an infant."

Another said, "It was the song my little sister liked the best, the one who drowned in the lake."

There was silence again. And then the oldest of the ancestors said, "Girl, what do you want?" Sabulana said, "Ancestors, we are starving. We do not know why. Tell us what you did to raise crops that was different from what we do now."

The ancestors leaned forward. "Only because your song recalls our human life to us," the oldest mother said, "will we tell you. We do not interfere with your lives. We leave you alone and, in return, you remember us with fondness and some fear."

Sabulana bowed to the oldest mother. "But will you help us now? Tell us what to do?"

There was a silence. Then another ancestor spoke. "Do you remember to leave the corners of the fields unplowed?"

Sabulana looked up at her, puzzled. "Why? The extra crops that grow there. . . ." Then she remembered that no crops were growing at all.

A second ancestor spoke. "And do you always rest and worship the goddess of Earth on Thursdays?" Sabulana shook her head. "Thursday is a day like any other."

There was silence. "The wild beasts—do you kill them with love and care? Do you always remember they are living creatures like yourselves?" another asked.

"The giraffes? The antelope? Those dumb elephants? They do not know what people know . . ." Sabulana was answering the questions rapidly when she felt the eyes of her ancestors on her. Slowly she began to realize what they were asking.

"Are those the things you did?" she demanded.

The oldest of ancestors spoke again. "You transgress against the rules of our mother, the Earth. No wonder you are starving. Why should she feed such rude children? You must follow her ways again."

Sabulana nodded. She remembered, just barely, how she used to play in the sun on the Thursday holiday. She remembered people praying over their meals of meat, thanking the animals that died for their food. And she remembered those little bird-filled corners where she played hide-and-seek, there in the fields. So that had been the reason!

"Now," said the oldest elder, "you must go. You are near to dying. If you stay here, you cannot even become a ghost like us, for you have had no children and cannot be an ancestor. Hurry. Get back to your village. Pray with your people."

Sabulana hopped and crawled across the field to the village. She was, indeed, growing weaker. She pulled herself along, feeling the strength dying in her legs. After falling several times and pulling herself to her feet, she reached the round houses of the village.

"Listen," she began to yell, but a wave of dizziness hit her. She held herself up on her staff. Curious, everyone at their doorsteps looked up at her. But they were too weak to move.

"We have wronged our mother, the Earth!" Sabulana said, as loudly as she could manage. "We are starving because she is angry."

Sabulana began to sway with exhaustion and hunger. As people looked on, she fell to the ground. "Is she dead?" a person nearby asked, not really caring, because so many died these days.

But Sabulana did not die. Lying on the ground, she had a vision. Before her she saw the Earth goddess, a giant woman with a kindly face. And she saw the ancestors, kneeling before the goddess. She could hear them begging for the goddess to forgive the people of her village, to give them another chance. And she saw a smile light the goddess's face as she nodded.

Sabulana fainted. When she came to, someone was holding water to her mouth. She drank, then opened her eyes wide at what she saw.

Everywhere trees were hanging with fresh fruit. Children were pulling berries off low-hanging bushes and stuffing them into their mouths. The gardens were growing so fast she could almost hear the swish of the plants as they pushed up through the soil. Animals were walking up to the hunters, who shot them in amazement.

Sabulana's eyes closed again, but this time it was in happy sleep. When she awoke, she called everyone in the village together again and instructed them as the ancestors had said.

"We must leave the corners of the fields unplowed," she told them. "And we must not work on Thursdays. And we must not ever kill animals for sport. Everything that lives is part of the great Earth, and if we hurt one part we hurt ourselves."

The people stood around Sabulana, eager to learn and to assure themselves of continued food. When Sabulana had finished her speech, the oldest woman of the village came forward.

"Child," the old one said in a croaking voice, "you have saved our lives. Our chief is usually a woman with many years, someone whom we can rely on to tell us what we need to hear. But you have done the chief's job in this time. And so you must remain our leader."

Sabulana's people began to cheer. The elder who had proclaimed her chief brought necklaces of silver and hung them on Sabulana. Then she wrapped her hair in a beautiful scarf. The young girl stood up, straight and proud. She took a deep breath. "Thank you," she said simply. "Thank you, my people."

• • •

# Goddesses of Africa

Africa is huge, a continent second only to Asia in size. More than 700 million people live there, speaking 800 languages and representing 3,000 ethnic groups. It is therefore hard to discuss "African" concepts of the goddess as a whole, for there are Ashanti, Yoruba, Ibo, Fulani, Mandingo, Hausa, Dogon, Masaai, Zulu—and many other—ways of describing her. In addition, there are many spiritual traditions in South, Central, and North America that are derived from African religions, brought over on the slave ships by people who held her dear. We find Oshun, for instance, appearing in both Africa and the New World as a goddess of love and desire, and still competing with motherly Oya for the thunder god Chango. Ymoja, too, appears in both areas as queen of waters. In Africa itself we find Abuk, the first woman, who discovered how we can feed ourselves from the produce of earth; the sky princess Andriam-Vabi-Rano; the mischievous girl Chichinguane; and hundreds more, each with her own vivid myth and her own ceremonial tradition.

Common to African religions is reverence for the ancestors. The ancient mothers and fathers become something like gods and goddesses—more than spirits or ghosts—full of power and strength. Honoring the ancestors is an important part of many African religions, as it is of many religions in other areas of the globe.

In addition, African religion tended to honor the earth that feeds and sustains us. Among the Ashanti people of Western Africa, the goddess Asase Yaa ruled the earth and all its produce. Without her assistance, there would be no food, for it was only the goodwill of Mother Earth that provided sustenance for her children. Traditional Ashanti belief demands that reverence for earth be the primary goal of all humans. There were ways of showing this reverence: for instance, a farmer would leave a little patch of unplowed earth in each field, to signify that Asase Yaa merely loans use of the land to humans. And farmers also give the earth a holiday from plowing and hoeing every Thursday, to show that they care for her health and well-being. In return, Mother Earth provides us all we need to eat, and she takes us back to herself when we die.

# Honoring Your Heritage

No matter what your ethnic or national background, you will find a spiritual tradition unique to it that honors feminine strength. All cultures have, at some point, honored a goddess or a female figure with goddesslike powers. Some of these are converted into saints with the coming of new religions, while others can be found in fairy tales and other stories told to children. Goddesses come in every shape, size, color, and height. You will be able to find goddesses like yourself with just a little searching.

It is good spiritual practice to familiarize yourself with the goddesses of your own people. Like many Americans, you may be a mixture of many ethnic groups, which gives you even more goddesses to choose from. How do you find the goddesses of your clan? Check the further reading list at the back of this book to start. Then read anything you can find that describes the ancient ways of your people. Learn the geography, the climate, and the major landmarks as well as the human history. And remember that, because the goddess has been hidden for many years, the search may not always be an easy one. However, more and more information is made available every year on the subject, so consider your research effort an ongoing one.

Talk, as well, to your older relatives. If they are made anxious or uneasy by words like "goddess" and "pagan," use milder words. Ask about folklore and folktales. Ask about old customs and holidays. Most of them arose in the pagan past and represent the ties of your ancestors to the land of your heritage. You may still be celebrating some pagan ways within your family. Food, for instance, tends to remain a constant at holidays. A Scandinavian family may make "lucia cats" on Christmas morning, little muffins to celebrate the holiday. These originated as ways of honoring the sun goddess at her darkest time. Similarly, the potato pancakes or latkes of eastern European Jewish families have their origin in foods eaten to keep the Hag of Winter away at the winter solstice. You may already be practicing goddess rituals with your family!

Songs, festival clothing, daily rituals—all these can carry ancient goddess information from your family's past to you today. Learn as much as you can about them, and incorporate them into your practice.

After you have learned about your own heritage, you are ready to begin exploring other cultures. It is important, in doing so, to be aware of the opinions of those who have traditionally held these beliefs, and to engage respectfully in your search for knowledge. Many American Indian people, for instance, discourage non-Indians from practicing traditional Native American ceremonies on land that has been stolen from the original inhabitants. Other ancient ways may have been traditionally practiced only on certain days or by initiated individuals. Do not assume that, just because you like a ceremony, it is yours to celebrate.

A good rule to follow is: if you are giving nothing back for the knowledge, it is not yours. If you wish to learn Native American ways, think about contributing to that society as a volunteer or by doing fundraising drives. Another good rule is that you should wait to be offered an opportunity to participate in ceremonies that are not yours by heritage. The spiritual world is not a shopping mall. Just because you want something does not mean you necessarily can have it. Learning to live with respect for others is part of the Wild Girl path.

## Toning, Chanting, and Singing

Use of the voice is an important part of most spiritual traditions. Think about Christmas carols. In the middle of every winter, we hear them played over loudspeakers, sung by choirs, and hummed by our friends and family. They help set the mood for the holiday. But they also remind us of the mythic story that is enacted in that yearly festival of the little child born to the virgin mother, a miracle baby who saves the world. Even if you are not Christian, you grow to know the story through songs sung every year.

Before recorded music was invented, all music was live music, made in the moment by musicians and singers you could see as they performed. People sang for pleasure more often, when there was no radio or CD player to provide music. Using your own voice to make music is different than only using your ears to listen to it. There is great pleasure in singing, even if just in the bath or shower. This primary human joy has become more and more distant from us, however, as we have come to rely on recordings by professional musicians and singers. Who wants to sing when you can hear a beautiful, trained voice, so much better than your own?

But the spirit expresses itself in song, as it does in dance. Singing connects us, through our breath, with the world around us. Just listening is not the same. Making toning, chanting, and singing part of your spiritual practice is an important part of the goddess path.

Even for people who say, "But I can't carry a tune," toning is an excellent way to use the voice in ritual and meditation. Toning is very simple to do and, because it is extremely effective in centering the mind and producing a slightly altered state of consciousness, it is used for raising power in many spiritual circles.

Breathe deeply for a few moments, letting the breaths be long and slow. Then, begin to sound the breaths. Do not force a note; just let your voice sing a slow "ahhhhhh" note until you run out of breath. Do this again and again, extending the tone as long as you can each time. If you have a number of people toning together, you will notice that your tones shift slightly in response to the tonal changes of others around you. Again, do not force a tone or change in tone. Even if there are some points of discord, let your voice carry the notes just as they come out.

Chanting is another form of power-raising that can be very effective. In chanting, you repeat a short song over and over and over. You may want to chant for as much as a half-hour each time. Some short chants are given in this chapter. You can write your own or gather some from books and recordings. A chant is usually only two to four lines long. It may have various verses or changing words. The point is the repetition, which creates a meditative mood in the singer.

Finally, there are spiritual songs. These are longer than chants, and sometimes more musically complicated. They are used in rituals and meditations to carry the seasonal mood or theme of the ritual. There are hundreds of possibilities for each purpose, or you may choose to write your own. Setting your own magical words to music can be a very empowering experience for a woman on the Wild Girl path. Or you may wish to write new words to a familiar melody. Lift up your voice and sing to the strength and beauty that is within you and in the world.

# A Wild Girl Songbook

There are many appropriate songs for rituals and meditation that can be found on CDs and tapes. Look especially in the New Age and World Music sections. Some will be labeled with "pagan" or "women's" labels, while others will not. There is also an increasing number of songs from popular music that reflect an earth-honoring and woman-positive vision. You may also wish to look into music that reflects your ethnic heritage. Be sure to look for music that affirms the womanly part of your identity. Songs that mock women's power are never appropriate for those on a spiritual journey.

Here are some well-known chants that are used by many ritual groups. All are by anonymous poets and musicians. When you sing them, let your heart be grateful for their gifts to you.

Reprinted by kind permission of Julie Forest Middleton from *Songs For Earthlings* (Emerald Earth Publishing, 1998).

### *The Earth Is Our Mother*

## *I Will Be Gentle with Myself*

I will be gen-tle with my-self, I will love my-self. I am a child of the u-ni-verse, be-ing born each mo-ment.

## *Earth My Body*

Earth my bod-y, wa-ter my blood, air my breath and fire my spir-it.

## *May Artemis Protect You*

May Ar-te-mis pro-tect you, and He-ra pro-vide you, and the wo-man-soul with-in you guide your way home.

## Rise Up, O Flame

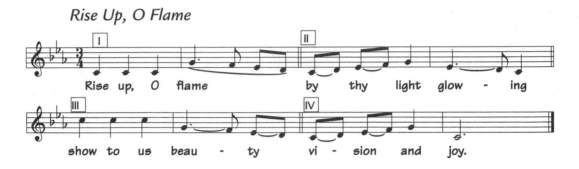

Rise up, O flame by thy light glow - ing

show to us beau - ty vi - sion and joy.

## Wearing My Long Wing Feathers

Arapaho Ghost Dance Song

Wear - ing my long wing feath - ers as I fly,

wear - ing my long wing feath - ers as I fly, I

cir - cle a - round, I cir - cle a - round, the boun - daries of the Earth.

## Activities for Brave Wild Girls

 Create an ancestor altar on which you place pictures of female ancestors, or their names written out on paper, or symbols of their talents. To do this, you will have to ask members of your family questions about your ancestors. These can be distant ancestors—even those in the "old country" or the continent of origin. They can also be near ancestors, whose memory still lives. When you begin your meditations and rituals, thank your ancestors for the gifts and talents they bestowed upon you.

 Create a songbook of heritage songs. Within every heritage, there are songs that express ancient wisdom. Find recordings and books of songs from your country or countries of origin. Learn them, and write the words down in your spiritual diary or in a separate book. Continue to expand this book as you continue on your spiritual journey.

 Take a trip—either real or virtual—to the land(s) of your origin. If your family travels, or your school offers travel-study, travel to the land of your ancestors. Experience the way the light falls on the hills, the way the plants scent the air, the way the stars look overhead. If you are not able to travel, read about and look at videorecordings of others' trips. Learn the names of the mountains and the rivers and the other important geographical features.

 Write a litany to the ancestors. A litany is a list-prayer, in which each line has a similar grammatical shape. You might say, "Thank you ancestors, for my (smile, or strong legs, or memory)." Use your own words, and make your list as long and comprehensive as possible. If you remember a relative, now deceased, who had the same talents or bodily features as you do, you may want to alter the litany to include them: "Thank you, grandmother, for my blue eyes." If you have bodily features that embarrass you, find ways to offer thanks for them as well, for they may be helpful parts of your inheritance without your realizing it: "Thank you, grandfather, for my short legs that keep me near to Mother Earth." Accepting all of our heritage can be a challenge, but it is an important part of our paths.

 Write a letter to your descendents. Imagine a young woman 200 years from now, your great-great-granddaughter. Tell her what you hope she will inherit from you. Tell her what you have learned in your spiritual quest so far. Send her a blessing from you, her ancestor.

# 11

# *Midwife to Herself*

## Greece

Leto was pregnant. Her belly was huge, big enough to hold twins. She walked unsteadily, rolling with each step. Her sister Asteria walked beside her, offering an arm when Leto looked too weary to go on.

The women had been walking for weeks. They no longer remembered where they had been, but sometimes they stumbled upon a familiar village and realized that they had walked in a huge circle, coming back to where they had started. But they could not stop, except to steal moments of exhausted sleep in the shade of an olive grove. Too long, and they would hear the hiss of the snake that slithered along in their wake. Too long, and it would slip between them and bite at their feet with its fangs.

They usually took turns sleeping, one always on guard. The snake appeared at the moment of the curse, the curse that had kept Leto pregnant for months past her time, growing steadily larger. From the sky they heard the words, "No place where the sun shines will welcome you to bear your child!" Leto had offended a divinity who lived far up in the mountains, and for that offense, she had been cursed.

Without her sister, Leto would have died—and her child inside her—long ago. But Asteria foraged for their meals and kept watch while Leto napped. She prayed constantly, hoping that heaven's will could be altered. And she walked beside her sister, always with a helpful word or a helping hand.

Labor pains had come and gone. One time the women were in the deep shade of a huge mountain. Asteria stood guard, hoping to fend off the huge serpent, when Leto began to pant and scream. But the child did not descend through the birth canal—perhaps because there was still a little light, because perhaps the sun could see her pain. So Asteria looked for dark shapes in the hillsides that might be caves. She found one, but it was too high for Leto to climb. A few weeks later, another cave made its location known by the darkness of its mouth. This one was reachable, and Asteria helped her sister up the steep hill and into the cool damp space.

There they rested for a time, alert for the snake who never seemed far away. But this time, they seemed to have escaped its stealthy tracking. Leto, her face running with sweat from the climb, grabbed her belly suddenly. The labor pains had begun again. Deep in a cave where no daylight had ever been seen, it seemed she would finally bear her child.

But just at that moment, from the rear of the cave, the massive head of the serpent struck out. The snake was longer than either of the women, its head wider than theirs. With its mouth open, it could swallow a whole leg at one bite. But it did not choose to devour them. Instead, the snake tormented them, biting them hard on the legs and arms, writhing over their bodies and choking them, so that they fled the cave as they had fled every other place of apparent safety.

For more months they wandered. Leto grew so big she could no longer walk, not even holding her belly with her hands or leaning heavily on her sister's arms. Now Leto crawled, dragging her huge body with her weakening arms. Finally the day came when she could not move.

They were near the ocean. The sun was blazing hot, and the water looked cool and blue. Knowing the snake would soon be upon them, the sisters sat, resting against each other and staring out to sea.

They heard the slippery sound of the snake as it slithered through the nearby grasses. Asteria took her sister's hand. They could go no farther. They would have to accept being eaten alive by the monster.

The snake slunk up to them and began to wrap itself around Leto's leg. Her eyes widened in terror and pain, but she had no voice left with which to cry out. Asteria grabbed a stone and tried to batter the snake's skull, but it turned on her and began to tear strips of flesh from her arm. Bleeding, desperate, Asteria grabbed Leto's arm and dragged her into the sea. "Perhaps he cannot follow here!" she said to her frightened sister. "Or at least, drowning is better than being eaten alive!" But the snake followed them, stretching out in great writhing leaps from the shore, biting at Leto's arms as she struggled to escape. Asteria pulled Leto further and further out into the water, until she had stepped off the shoreline shelf and plummetted into the depths of the sea. Leto watched in horror as the snake grew closer and as her sister disappeared into the blue waters.

But that was not, in fact, what had happened. Asteria had begun to change. Her body grew flat and wide, then flatter and wider, then even flatter and wider until she had no human features at all. She floated there, a sunken island of flesh, just below the surface of the water. Leto, not knowing what else to do, leaped onto the island that had been her sister.

The snake could not reach her now, and she could keep her head just enough above water to breathe. And instantly, her labor pains began again. She was finally resting in a place where the sun did not shine, for although the light fell on the water's surface, it did not reach the lower depths where Asteria floated. Swift and hard the pains came, shaking Leto's body violently. She felt rushes of warmth between her legs as her watery amniotic fluid flowed into the ocean. She could barely keep on her feet with the violence of her contractions, but she waved her arms frantically to stay afloat.

With a great surge, something broke free of her. Before Leto knew what was happening, a girl stood beside her, still bloody and red from birth. Her long stay in the womb had allowed Artemis to grow much larger than a normal child. And because of her divine blood, she was fully mature at birth.

Artemis knew exactly what to do. First she took a gulp of air, then swam down to bite the umbilical cord that tied her to her mother, tying it off quickly before she bled to death. Then Artemis propped her mother up on her sturdy body while pressing at Leto's now-sagging belly. Leto did not know it, but another child rested within. Unless that child were born quickly, the serpent would reach Leto and strangle or bite her to death.

Artemis gasped for breath and dived under the water again. Swimming between her mother's legs, she grabbed the head of the child just as it began to emerge. With all her strength, she helped pull the oversized child free and swam with him to the surface, where she once again bit the cord and tied it off expertly.

The child was gasping for breath, and so was Leto. Beneath their feet, the island that had been Asteria had begun to grow again. Now that the children were born, the curse was lifted. Asteria's flesh hardened into rock and pushed out of the sea until it formed an island, the sacred island of Delos in the seas of Greece. There the persecuted Leto raised her twin children, the moon goddess Artemis and the sun god Apollo. Although Asteria never returned to human form, Leto felt comforted by the presence underfoot of her devoted sister. The children grew up strong and bold and free.

It was from Delos that Artemis finally traveled to make her own life in the wilderness of Arcadia. There, the girl who had been her own midwife gathered around her bands of strong young girls. They spent their days hunting with bow and arrow in the green-wood, running barelegged and barefoot with their lean hunting hounds. They bathed together in the fresh cold springs of the forest, laughing as they related the day's exploits and teasing each other. And, whenever they found an animal suffering the pains of birth, they called for their leader Artemis, who though never a mother herself knew everything to do to ease a female animal's suffering.

And they still live there, Artemis and her Wild Girls—in every wilderness and forest in the world, and in each of our hearts too, when we are as strong and brave and free as they are.

• • •

# Goddesses of Greece

In many books of mythology, the goddesses of Greece are described in great detail; they are also mentioned in poetry, pictured in art, and otherwise are made part of our culture. Even on television today, references to Greek mythology abound: the jealous Hera of the television program *Hercules* is one such example, as is the Amazon tribe from which Xena's mate Gabrielle hails. Greek mythology is given so prominent a place in European culture that it is easy to believe it is somehow more important, even superior, to other mythologies.

But that is not the case. The Greeks had a splendid pantheon of goddesses and gods, it is true, and some great literature about their feats. But Egyptian, Japanese, Ojibway, Irish, and many other mythologies have characters as exciting and stories as compelling as the Greeks had. Enjoy what they offer, but learn others as well, especially those of your own heritage.

For every aspect of a woman's life, Greek mythology offers at least one divine image. Artemis was goddess of girls. They danced before her image at Brauronia, wearing saffron-colored dresses and moving like bears. She was goddess of the wilderness, whose power was seen in the natural order of the moon as it turned in its phases across the sky. She was also the midwife goddess who nurtured both human and animal young and their mothers.

But she was only one of the many goddesses the Greeks loved. Aphrodite was the goddess of love and art, a beautiful goddess who makes lovers find each other beautiful. Hera was the goddess of womanhood's three phases as girl, mother, and crone. Athena was the helmeted goddess of wisdom, Psyche the butterfly goddess of the soul, Demeter the grain goddess, Circe the enchantress. From their tiny, ragged peninsula in southern Europe, the Greeks seeded the world with beautiful, vibrant, powerful goddesses. In learning about their myths and images, we can be thankful for the great wisdom of that ancient people.

# Welcome to Womanhood

Many—perhaps most—cultures have had a special ritual that was celebrated when a girl became a woman. Usually this was at her first menstrual period, which marked her as able to bear children and enter the second stage of a woman's life. Some of these rituals were extremely elaborate and complex, with singing and dancing and feasting. Others were simpler, often involving a retreat to a sacred place so that the girl could learn from older women about her new life's possibilities and could grow familiar with her own body's changes.

It may seem hard to believe, in today's society, that there was a time when a girl's first blood was celebrated with parades and parties. Wouldn't that be embarrassing, having everyone know? But, far from being unusual, such events were common. And far from being a source of pain and humiliation, these events were looked forward to, and remembered, in the same way today's brides think of their weddings. In some areas of the world, girls still celebrate their initiation into womanhood as a happy public event, with their change in status and physical capability known and recognized by everyone in their village.

For almost all women in contemporary urban society, however, the first blood is not noted. The change from girlhood to womanhood is hidden. And this has meant that both girlhood and womanhood lose some of their power. Little girls are painted up to look like adults, and adult women try to look young. Women's bodies are used to sell cars, but the natural processes of those bodies is spoken of as shameful and disgusting. Buying sanitary products can be a humiliating experience for a woman. Why? We are not embarrassed by buying food—we even eat in public. And bleeding is as natural an act as eating.

Reclaiming the first blood as an important stage in a woman's life is only one part of a contemporary movement to honor woman's power and strength. Only a few decades ago, women who ran and competed athletically were viewed as peculiar, even threatening. Now we see women athletes everywhere. Just a hundred years ago, women were considered too stupid to vote. Now politicians court the votes of women.

In the same way, women were only a few years ago banished from religion, allowed to sit in the pews but never to be a priestess. This has changed. Women-honoring religions are the fastest-growing spiritual movements in America. Whether they be called Wiccan or witchcraft or pagan, these movements are demanding that women's realities become part of spirituality again—as they were for hundreds of thousands of years, and as they remain in some areas of the world.

You, in following the path traced by the chapters of this book, have become part of that movement. Together with hundreds of thousands, perhaps millions, of other women and men, you are seeking a new vision of what it is to be a woman. You want to be sensitive as well as strong, smart as well as intuitive, powerful as well as loving. You want to be everything you can be. You want to be in a partnership with someone who respects you and honors you, but who loves you passionately as well. You do not assume you have to choose between having children and having a career. You do not assume that you can't speak for yourself as well as for others. You can pilot a space shuttle or save a baby animal. You are the first of a new breed—but you are exactly like all those great women who lived before you, who fought the same fights and dreamed the same dreams.

In following the Wild Girl path, you have found within yourself the knowledge and confidence to attain what you will. You can protect yourself when you need to. You can find peace and comfort in the earth's beauties. Now that you have done this inner and outer work, you are ready to claim your position as a full woman. Whether you have bled your first blood—or even if you first bled years ago—you can go through the magical portals to womanhood, through the ritual known as initiation.

## Women's Initiation Ceremonies

To undergo an initiation ceremony means to stand at the threshold of a change in life and to step consciously over it. To "initiate" means to start something. Yet initiation is also a conclusion. Something is left behind when we move forward across that threshold. In the case of initiation into womanhood, what is left behind is childhood.

But girlhood has its advantages! You can play while others work. You can dream without worrying about whether those dreams will ever come true. You can make playmates out of animals or flower fairies or anyone you please. You do not have to think about anything serious if you don't want to.

Why be eager to leave childhood behind? Why do we yearn to become adults, to join that world where play and dreams are irrelevant, unimportant, silly, where flower fairies do not exist, and where fun is something you get only if you have enough money?

Why rush ahead to such a world? Because children have no power in our world. We never ask children who should become president, although the president's actions today will determine the world they live in tomorrow. In fact, we do not even let children vote. We do not let children say "no" to war or abuse or violence, even though children—especially girl children—suffer the most from those tragedies. Children's wisdom is mocked, scoffed at, derided. "Kids say the darndest things." Who wants to be powerless in a world where power is everything?

In our hearts, we know that girlhood is an exciting place to be, despite our lack of power and our vulnerability. Even as we pass across the threshold into womanhood, we look back wistfully at that dreamy, playful being we once were, at the Wild Girl.

Initiation can allow you to hold on to the powers and pleasures of childhood while also growing into the responsibilities of womanhood. You do not have to give up being a Wild Girl. You just have to find a place for her in your new life as a Wild Woman. You can still be dreamy and free and full of energy and joy.

This is why the Greek girl initiates danced before Artemis, dedicating themselves to her. For that goddess is the epitome of the Wild Girl. She lives in the woods, surrounded only by her girlfriends. She is entirely self-sufficient, hunting her own food and protecting herself from anyone who might harm her. Yet she is endlessly helpful to other female creatures. It is Artemis who helps the suffering mother lion give birth safely. It is Artemis who raises the orphaned cubs if the mother cannot survive. She is both wild and nurturing, carefree and fiercely responsible. Her animal image is the bear, whom the Greek girls imitated in their initiation dance.

Only you can decide when the time is ripe for your initiation. Just because your Wild Girl friends have decided to take that step does not mean you need to accompany them. If you want to remain a girl for awhile longer, give yourself permission to do so. Embrace your girlhood's power fully before you decide to step across the threshold to womanhood. For although she remains forever within you, the Wild Girl may retreat for long periods while you learn to be a woman. Be certain that you are ready to take the big step to womanhood. Then, dance forward to your own powerful, new self.

## Your Own Initiation

This initiation ritual is based on the ancient Greek Artemis dedication that girls underwent at the age of nine or ten. Elements of contemporary Wiccan practice are also incorporated. Feel free to change any elements of the ritual that you like. The ritual is designed to be performed by a group, but can be adapted for a solo initiation as well.

Begin by building an Artemis altar. If you can find an image of the goddess—a sculpture or photograph—put that on the altar. Or use an image of a bear. Or any wild thing, from a tree branch to a vase of wildflowers. Each girl to be initiated should also select a representative object that she will place on the altar before the ritual. Also put on the altar a glass of pure water, a small dish of salt, and a dish of seeds and nuts.

Artemis rituals were generally performed at full moons, so select a full-moon night for this event. You may choose to invite people (mothers, siblings, friends) to witness the ritual, or perform it only with your Circle. Each girl to be initiated should dress in yellow, the color worn by Artemis's girls in the great rituals at Brauronia in ancient Greece. Also prepare yourself by getting drums, rattles, or other percussive instruments for every girl to be initiated. Other instruments can be played by members of the audience.

Assemble, standing around the altar in a circle, carrying your instruments. Begin by invoking the five directions: east for air and the mind; south for fire and the passions; west for water and the emotions; north for earth and the body; and the center for the soul. Ask the guardians of each of these directions to be with you during the ceremony. At the end of each invocation, you may wish to use the Wiccan words "blessed be," which means "we recognize the holiness of this moment."

Then raise power through toning (see chapter 10). Let the sound swell and grow loud. Continue for ten minutes, or as long as you can keep the energy high. When you feel as though you are sitting under a cone of power, begin whispering the Wild Girl goddess's name: ARTEMIS. Repeat it slowly, many times, together and separately. Let the power build again. When you feel the power is at a peak, begin drumming slowly, in rhythm to the goddess's name. Sway as you drum, until you cannot contain the energy of your dance any longer.

Then, begin to dance for the goddess. Pretend you are a bear, her totem animal. Shuffle your feet, sway back and forth, swing your head widely. Keep chanting the goddess's name. Keep beating the drum.

Each initiate will then dance her own individual dance. One at a time, put down your drum, close your eyes, and dance to the others' drumming. Picture, in your mind, a wide doorway opening before you. Dance your way through that opening. When you get to the other side, picture all your female relatives—all the way back to the beginning of time, to the great ancestral mother Eve, whose bones were found in Africa—standing there to greet you. Call out the names of those you know: "I join you—Mary—in womanhood. I join you—Margaret—in womanhood." When you run out of names, call them by their relationship to you. "I join you, great-great-grandmother, in womanhood." If you wish to make a famous woman one of your "ancestors," do so: "I join you, Marie Curie, in womanhood. I join you, Georgia O'Keeffe, in womanhood. I join you, Joan of Arc, in womanhood."

When you have named all the ancestors you wish to proclaim and honor, step back into the circle and let another woman come forward.

After each has named her ancestral mothers, slow down the beat and let it grow softer and finally silent. When the drums have finished, put them down and approach the altar. Pick up the glass or chalice of water from the altar, and pass it on to the next, saying, "May you drink deep of your womanhood." Then bless each other by pinching salt and throwing it over each others' shoulders, saying, "May you never doubt the blessing of our woman's blood." Finally, feed each other seeds, saying, "May the best seeds you have sown in your girlhood flower in your womanhood."

Conclude by thanking the goddess Artemis for her blessing upon your ritual. Then call again to each of the elements, thanking them for their part in the ritual and asking them to "go if you must, stay if you will." Finally, join hands and thank each other for witnessing the passage to a new stage of life.

## Activities for Initiated Wild Girls

 Learn about your body. As a woman, you have responsibility to care for yourself in the best possible way. This includes your sexual health. Take a class, or read a book, or watch a video about women's reproductive system. Remember too that sexuality is a gift of pleasure. Learn about how women experience pleasure. Make certain that you do not give your body to anyone who refuses to acknowledge your right to pleasure, safety, and health.

 Help another woman. There are women in your community who suffer because of homelessness, poverty, or other problems. Find out what possibilities exist for service in your area. Volunteer on a rape hotline, hold a coat drive for an Indian reservation, help at a soup kitchen. There is much to be done, and your Wild Girl energy will be welcome.

 Find a teacher. To continue to grow as a powerful woman, you need teachers. Your local women's bookstore or center will tell you about classes in women's spirituality. You may also find such classes at community colleges or universities; even if you are too young to enroll, you can often audit to gain the knowledge. Honor elders by listening to them, but honor them as well by offering them your own wisdom.

Go on a pilgrimage. Select a site that has spiritual significance for you or that honors a powerful woman. It could be a beautiful natural spot or a site of cultural importance. It need not be far away; someplace in your own town is as likely a spot for pilgrimage as someplace a world away. With your friends, take a trip there—not as tourists but as pilgrims. Meditate at the spot, then create a spontaneous ritual to honor its power.

 Talk to your mother. Now that you have passed the threshold into womanhood, your relationship with your mother will change. Some mothers will not find this easy to accept, as they fear losing their daughters. If you cannot talk to your mother directly, make an audiotape of your feelings and give it to her. Or write a series of poems in which you express your sense of womanhood. There may still be difficulties between you, but you have taken steps toward relating to her, woman to woman. If your mother is deceased or absent, or if she completely resists listening to you about your spiritual quest, never forget you have another mother: the great Earth itself. Find a peaceful place and confide in her. She is already listening to you.

· · ·

# 12

# *Starting a Wild Girls' Circle*

In the dim recesses of mountain caves, archaeologists have found traces of a circle dance—from 30,000 years ago. From the beginning of human history until today, humans have celebrated our spirituality together in song and dance, ritual and prayer. Women have always been participants, and often leaders, in this human endeavor.

As you walk along the path of the Wild Girl, you may feel inspired to gather friends to join you in this quest and this celebration. While it is possible to celebrate your womanhood in solitude, working with a group has its own special power. There may be a group already in existence in your area that honors the goddess and in which you might participate. Such groups are generally relatively diverse, sometimes including men, usually including women of many ages. In addition or in place of such a group, you may wish to organize others like yourself into a Wild Girls' Circle. This chapter offers you suggestions on making your Wild Girls' Circle successful.

# Gathering the Circle

Gathering the members of your circle is the first, and perhaps the most important, step you will take. A circle can consist of only two or three people. It can include as many as thirteen, the traditional number for a coven. But the number of participants is less important than their willingness to work together and their commitment to the process of spiritual development. Circle members must also be willing to engage in ritual activities together. Anyone who feels that this might create problems for them with their parents' religion, or who feels uncomfortable exploring this aspect of spirituality, can function as an associate member, joining you for discussions but not for activities.

Start the process of gathering your Wild Girls' Circle by talking about the ideas in this book with your friends and acquaintances. Look for those who are willing to meet once a month for a year. Using this book as a guide, spend one month on each chapter, culminating with a group initiation into womanhood. You may continue meeting after you have completed your initiation. Suggestions for ongoing activities are at the end of this chapter.

The Wild Girl way is not for everyone. It is not a shortcut to looking like Sabrina nor a way to gain status or power or popularity. It is, however, one of the most exciting experiences you can have, because it offers you an opportunity to explore your potential as a woman on all planes: physical, emotional, intellectual, and spiritual. It joins you to the millions of women who have embraced their womanhood deliberately, with ritual and in the company of other women.

Your Wild Girls' Circle should be limited to young women. You may define "young" however you wish. What you are seeking is women who are alike in their stage of development. A young women who is just approaching the onset of menstruation will have different needs and feelings than one who is about to enter college, yet both are young and can benefit from exploring the Wild Girl path. But older women may have forgotten the beginning of their journey to womanhood. They may make light of—or take too seriously—your special circumstances. They may attempt to mother you at a time when you are learning to mother yourself.

If you are an older woman considering the issues raised in this book, you may well benefit from spending a year on the Wild Girl path. Because we have no formal, generally recognized rituals of initiation into womanhood, even women who have substantial experience in spirituality have probably been denied this important rite of passage. Thus a group of older women may choose to celebrate, among themselves, the cycle given in this book.

It is possible for such older women to join with young relatives and friends—nieces, grandchildren, students—for this search. Many of the activities are enjoyable to engage in with women of varying ages. However, a balance of younger and older women is important, as is some time spent in separated age groups. Older women need time to process their grief at the lost girl within, something that their younger colleagues do not experience. Younger women need privacy in which to share their own realities without fear of being judged or overly protected. A joint older-younger group that celebrates ritual and activities together, but that separates for discussion and sharing, can be very healing for all involved. A separate chapter offers suggestions for such a mixed group (see "Maiden/Mother MoonCircle").

Wild Girls' Circles should be limited to women. Many spiritual groups are open to people of both sexes, but your own womanhood is best explored in the company of other women. Would you really talk openly about your fears and desires in the presence of boys or men? Probably you would either keep silent or exaggerate, to gain or hide from their attention. At this stage in your life, celebrating only with other women is important. After you have passed through your initiation, you may choose to include men in your circle. But for this year, find your circle companions among other women.

In selecting your circle companions, try to set aside racial, economic, appearance, and other prejudices. A Wild Girls' Circle is not an occasion to laugh at another's differing clothing styles, ethnic traditions, or ways of expression. You can gain immeasurably from knowing, in the intimate space of a spiritual community, young women of other races, classes, ethnic backgrounds, or religious traditions. Look around your neighborhood and your school, trying to be alert to and aware of the inner potential of the girls you encounter. Just because someone is popular does not make her a good choice for your group; she could be shallow and self-centered and mean-spirited. Just because a girl is not popular does not mean you should exclude her; she may have values and talents that are not obvious in the competitive and stressful world of today's schools. A rich family or cute figure does not guarantee that a girl will be a spirited Wild Girl companion. In selecting your circle, look beyond appearance and clothing and wealth.

Once you have found a group of young women willing to work together for a year, locate a place to meet. You will need somewhere private and safe. A large space is not necessary, but a room with a door you can close is. You need a place you can meet for several hours without interruption. Perhaps one of your members is able to provide space in her home. Perhaps you will meet in several homes alternatively. You might also ask for space at a school or a community center, a park district or a women's center.

Once you have established your location, select a meeting schedule. In keeping with the ancient belief that the new moon is a good time to plant spiritual seeds, you might meet on the night of that moon phase; this will vary month to month, however, so you might wish to set a standard meeting day—say, the first Wednesday—to simplify things. Establish a phone tree (each person calling two other designated people) so that, if there is bad weather or another problem that forces a schedule change, you can quickly contact each other.

Finally, before you begin meeting as a circle, have several meetings to establish guidelines for what you wish to do together. Agree on ground rules of behavior. Set your schedule of meetings for the year. Determine where the meetings will be held. Determine who will do what work for the circle. When these issues have been settled, you are ready to begin.

## The Meeting Format

After you have gathered your circle and set a meeting time, you are ready to begin your journey. Ask everyone to honor the starting time, and always allow some catch-up time to reestablish your connections with each other before you begin the meeting. But do not let the catching-up take time away from your Wild Girl work. Gossip and sharing can occur after the meeting as well as at other times.

Open each meeting with a simple ritual to center your energies. You can create your own ritual or adapt one from a book in the further reading section. Or you can use the following simple ritual: gather in a circle, either seated or standing. Light a candle in silence. Then join hands and begin humming quietly, letting the sound continue for five minutes or so (see chapter 10 for more information about toning to raise power). Let the toning slowly subside, then ask the goddess for her blessing on your circle and on your activities. Leave the candle burning throughout your meeting.

Limit the time of your meetings. If you wind up meeting for five hours one month, you may face the next meeting with dread. An hour or ninety minutes is plenty of time. Respect the circle and your companions by not leaving early unless absolutely necessary.

Begin each meeting by reporting on the activities of the previous month and sharing anything you have created. At the first meeting, each member can take her time to describe what has drawn her to the Wild Girl path. Let each circle member take her turn to speak for five to ten minutes. Each member should get the same amount of time; the less talkative will thus not be left feeling like they do all the listening, while the more talkative will not feel annoyed at having to keep the conversation going. While each member speaks, the others should remain in silence. There should be no cross-talk or interruption. It is important to let each Wild Girl have her own sacred time in the circle.

After the sharing time, read the goddess story for the month. Take turns reading; pass the book around, or let each read from her own book. Each reader can read a page or so, then let the next begin. After the reading, take a few moments to reflect upon the goddess and her myth. Going around the circle, each member then offers a short comment on how she relates to the story. What personal experiences does it remind you of? What emotions does it rouse in you? What fears and hopes?

After this sharing, join hands again in silence. Ask if anyone has a special need for healing; if so, focus on that member in silence for a few moments. If anyone has a special problem that is likely to affect them this month, this is the time to mention it and ask for help from the circle. There is no need to go into detail, or even into specifics; a member can just say, "I have a hard month coming up." After everyone who needs to has spoken, repeat together the following prayer three times: "Goddess of a thousand names, be with us." Close by blowing out the candle. But do not just run off at the end of the ritual portion of the meeting. Spend the next hour sharing personal news and celebrating with your circle. Discuss the events of the previous month in the context of what you are discovering about woman's power and strength.

During the month between meetings, see your Wild Girl friends for various events and activities. Do not, however, gossip or joke about anything that happened within your sacred circle. If someone has brought up a painful experience as part of your time together, do not mention it to her. She may wish to talk about the problem or situation, but she may not. Initiating discussion is entirely her privilege. Do not offer advice outside the circle. What is spoken there is secret; do not mention it to anyone outside the circle. Never discuss one member's experiences with another. Gossip can destroy a spiritual circle just as it can destroy a social one.

There are many activities in each chapter that will take your time during the month between meetings. Some are designed to be done alone; others can be done with companions. Remember to respect the diversity of members' experiences as you work through these activities. There should be no competition among members in doing these activities. There is no "right way" to do the activities; if a member comes up with an inventive interpretation that fits her needs, applaud her for her initiative. Sharing the results of the month's activities provides you an opportunity to get to know each other deeper, and to support each other's progress along the path.

## Nourishing the Circle

Now that you know what you are going to do at your Wild Girl meetings, the question has probably come to your mind: who does it? Nourishing a spiritual circle takes work. How do you make sure that the work all gets done?

There are several organizational models to choose from. One person can be high priestess, in charge of everything. Or there can be several such high priestesses. But though it sounds exciting to be a high priestess, it entails a lot of work and can exhaust people. It is far better to divide the work among several people. To do this, have each person keep the same position for the whole year or change duties every few months. However you decide to handle the division of duties, here are the positions you will need to fill:

**Organizer:** Makes sure there is a safe and convenient place for the meetings; organizes food or other treats for afterward; gets altar and ritual materials together.

**Ritualist:** Asks individuals to take special roles in ritual; writes liturgies for various events; finds readings and songs when appropriate.

**Counselor:** Attends to the interpersonal dynamics of the group; makes sure no one takes up more than her share of time or fails to take her turn; encourages positive nonritual interactions, and speaks with anyone who is disruptive to group process.

**Fool:** Makes sure that everyone is having fun.

For a circle with fewer than four people, some of the roles can be combined; in a group of more than four, some roles can be shared. Each one of us has some talents that fit us to one or more roles rather than others. It is best if everyone takes on all roles during the year, so that everyone has practice with the roles required to make the group work. However, do not switch more frequently than every three months, so that those fulfilling circle roles have an opportunity to learn them and perform them well.

In addition to making certain that all necessary group and ritual roles are satisfied, there will be other challenges you face as a group. If you expect that you will all get along perfectly with no arguments for the whole year, you will surely be disappointed. But if you view the difficulties as part of the learning you need to successfully walk the Wild Girl path, you can turn any occasion into a positive one. It is important for every member to truly honor the commitment to be together for a year, and to understand that the others will be similarly committed. This means that there can be no threats to banish someone from the circle nor to quit in order to punish someone. Similarly, maintaining the rules that circle members cannot gossip about what is shared in the circle will keep many problems at bay.

But what if someone refuses to follow the guidelines that the group has agreed to? If someone consistently skips meetings, comes late or leaves early, gossips outside the group, or disrupts the ritual, then it is necessary to confront that person and ask that the behavior change. Offer the feedback in as nonconfrontational a manner as possible. Sometimes the member may be unaware of the behavior or of its effect. Sometimes there are differing expectations that can be worked through. Sometimes there has been a simple mistake or misapprehension in what is expected.

When having such discussions, do not engage in "always" and "never" name-calling. Instead, describe a specific incident and its effect. Do not extend the discussion to things outside the group—to events at school or in the family or in other contexts. If you are the one being asked to change a behavior, try not to respond or excuse yourself. Simply hear what the problem is, meditate upon it, and consider whether you think the difficulty stems from another's problem or your own. If, for instance, one person gets very anxious when another is flippant about sexuality, both can learn from the difficulty: the frightened one can begin to encounter her own fears that need healing, and the flippant one can become aware of the reactions of others to her means of expression. Keeping the spiritual nature of the group's activities at the forefront of your discussion is important. This is not about "right" and "wrong," but about human understanding.

However, you may find some conflicts unresolvable. If you find yourself continually unhappy with the way you are treated in a group, especially if you feel emotionally blackmailed, manipulated, or otherwise made to feel unsafe, describe your feelings and ask to be released from your promise to remain with the group for a year. If the group refuses to hear your difficulty yet demands you stay, you have the right to decide that you cannot do so. Never withdraw from a circle without attempting to settle the problem. Never ask someone to leave a circle without attempting to settle the problem.

If members of your circle become at odds with each other, consider asking an older friend to meet with you to help you settle your differences. It is important that such a person not take sides, but work with everyone in the circle equally to try to discover what has caused the difficulty and how it can be settled. It is important that your circle not be a source of hurt or harm, but of healing.

## Sustaining the Circle

After meeting for a year and going through your initiation into womanhood, you have fulfilled your commitment to yourself and to your circle. But you may decide that you have gained enough spiritually that you wish to continue meeting together. At that point, you need to ask yourself the following questions:

- Do you wish to include new members?

- If so, how will they be chosen? What will be the expectations of new members? How will they be trained?

- If you include new members, should you only consider initiated young women?

- Do you wish to assist other women toward initiation, either through your own circle or by working with others? If so, how will you do this?

- Do you wish to admit men to your circle? If so, how will you select them?

- What will be your purpose in continuing to work together? Your previous goal was of initiation into womanhood. What other goals seem appropriate?

- How often will you meet? Will you celebrate the solar or lunar calender, or both?

- What forms will your ritual take?

It is possible that you may know of a group in your area whose philosophy is appropriate to all or some members of your group, in which case you may wish to join with them. Some members of your group may decide that the time is right for some solitary exploration. There should be no condemnation of anyone who, by listening to her spirit, decides to depart from your group, if it remains together; she should be made welcome to rejoin in the future.

Initiation into womanhood is only one step on the goddess path. There will be many, many more. But in working with other women to attain this initiation, you have learned the basic skills you need to continue in your spiritual quest. You have become aware of your dreams and your desires. You know how to make magic and how to honor the earth. You can create sacred space and protective ritual. You have become the midwife to your own growth and development. No matter what challenges and joys life offers you, you know that you have within you a Wild Girl, powerful and free and strong. She is your soul. Honor and praise her in all that you do.

. . .

# Appendix I
# Rites of Initiation

*Derise E. Tolliver, Ph.D.*

Derise E. Tolliver is a clinical psychologist who is a resident faculty member at the School for New Learning, DePaul University. Her professional and personal interests include African-centered psychology and the role of spirituality in education. Her passions include traveling to Africa, incorporating spirituality into her work and play, and helping people remember who they truly are. She can be reached at dtollive@wppost.depaul.edu.

It is Thursday, a sacred day for one of the important goddesses of a community in Ghana, West Africa. And Afua, a thirteen-year-old girl who lives in this community, is especially excited on this day. She has finally reached the age where she will go through the process that so many girls before her have experienced—initiation into womanhood. Although she has enjoyed the pleasures of childhood, playing with her friends and having little responsibility for household and family matters, Afua has now reached the point where she should be prepared for her life as an adult woman. It has been the tradition in her community for girls to go through a series of activities and processes, commonly known as rites of passage, in preparation for the next stage of their lives.

Afua is ready. The elder women and priestesses of the village are in charge of leading Afua and similarly aged girls through the initiation process. Early in the morning, the elders come by Afua's house and take her outside the village to a stream, where she and her agemates are to be bathed. This bath represents the beginning of the girls' transformation into womanhood. Afua's regular clothes are taken away; she and the other girls are all given bright red loincloths to wear. Their hairstyles will be changed later. The girls, or initiates as they are also called, are not allowed to speak to family or other villagers once the initiation process begins. They also have restrictions on their diet, based on foods that are associated with the goddess that the initiation is dedicated to. After the ritual bathing, the girls return to the village, where each of their families will have prepared a "farewell meal," accompanied by much singing and dancing, in anticipation of the "new woman" who will emerge in the next few days.

After the feast, the initiates are led to the home of a priest or the village chief, who will sprinkle holy water on them and say prayers. The girls are next led to a grove that contains the sacred stones of the village, known as *dipo* rocks. Here, the elder women will have each initiate sit on a rock, then get up, three times in a row, while saying, "Sit down, stand up, I make you a woman." After this ritual, Afua and the other girls will each be given a straw hat to wear, which indicates they have passed through another important phase of the initiation process.

The initiates return to the village. It is now that their intensive training will take place. This part of the process generally lasts four to seven days. The girls are still forbidden to talk to anyone. They are isolated from the rest of the village, while the elder women and priestesses teach them about what it means to be women—intuitive, imaginative, and wonderful people. They are put in touch with their creative power as childbearers, providers of food, and nurturers of the family and community. They are instructed about relating to each other and to men. Afua and her agemates will have no other responsibilities during this time period but to learn about being a woman in their society.

After the training period has successfully been completed, the initiates are newly presented to the village as women. Their straw hats are removed and decorative marks are placed on the top and sides of their face, almost like body painting. Their hair is washed, elaborately styled, and adorned, and they are dressed in brightly colored, patterned cloths, with many strands of beads draped around their necks and waists. Restrictions on their diet are lifted, and they are now allowed to speak again. Their families and the entire community come out to celebrate the initiates' achievement. Afua is now accepted as a woman in the community and can enjoy all the privileges that go along with her new status.

• • •

If you have joined a special club or organization that required you to go through certain steps before joining, you may already be familiar with the basic concept of initiation. Initiation is often described as an installation or inauguration process, that is, admitting someone into a group or club with a special or secret ceremony. However, in ancient and more traditional societies and cultures, the initiation is but one phase of a grander, more prolonged process referred to as rites of passage. This process is often sacred and spiritual because of the importance of these elements in people's daily lives. For these groups, one of the most important initiations occurs between childhood and adulthood. According to Malidome Some, an African healer, this type of initiation includes the young person in the community, and recognizes her genius while moving her toward maturity and adult responsibility. By going through the initiation process, the young girl is granted permission by her community to move to a higher level of social and educational development. This permission affirms that the girl has successfully completed the required steps in preparation for womanhood.

In traditional cultures, the rites of passage require that the initiate undergo certain challenges and rituals to gain the knowledge, maturity, and understanding that are required of a fully functioning woman. Initiation into adulthood—and specifically for girls, womanhood—is not just a matter of attaining the "legal" age to be an adult, as it is in most Western cultures. On the contrary, womanhood is a status and achievement that is not solely based on age; it is recognized by the larger community as a girl's readiness to take on the new responsibilities of adulthood.

The actual initiation is generally preceded by a preparation period, also known as a liminal phase, where the young girl is instructed by elder women on the ways of womanhood. This is an opportunity for the girl to learn what her community expects of her as an adult women. Initiations usually occur in a group of similarly aged or similarly developed girls. Often, they occur around the onset of puberty, as this marks developmentally so many changes in the lives of young women—physically, emotionally, and spiritually. During the rites of passage and initiation process, adult women in the community impart their knowledge and understanding of the wisdom, power, strength, and resulting responsibilities of womanhood. With the assistance of their elders, young girls come to acknowledge their connection to others within the community, while also embracing the importance of their own self-development. Often, the initiates will identify with a particular goddess or sacred object; the identification with the energy and characteristics of the goddess or object is thought to shape the future actions of the young women with meaning and purpose.

Initiations involve the use of rituals and symbols that are meaningful to both the girl being initiated and her community. For example, the ritual of calling in the four or six directions (north, south, east, and west, and possibly above and below) has been an important step in beginning initiations, since each direction represents aspects of nature and the life cycle. Pouring libations to acknowledge the Creator and ancestors and to ask for their blessings is often utilized in the beginning of initiation processes. These actions help to create a sacred space in which the initiation can take place. Ritual cleansing can also serve this purpose, through the use of burning sage or incense in the space and the washing of hands or bathing of the participants.

Colors, objects, sounds, and other items are often utilized symbolically in initiations. For example, white may be worn or used to decorate a space to signify purification and cleansing, while red might be used to signify the passion and aliveness of the new adult woman. Initiation ceremonies may occur at dawn or the new moon to symbolize the new beginning in the young girl's life. Ritual clothing, like a special dress, beads, or headwrap, can be worn to symbolize the transformation of the initiate.

The presence of challenges is a critical element of the initiation process. It is through the mastery of ordeals or completion of certain tasks that the girl "proves" she is ready to be a woman. By confronting the challenges faced during initiation, the young girl symbolically dies, followed by her rebirth as a woman. Again, these ordeals are often symbolic in nature. The girl may be asked to walk a straight line without faltering, to carry water without spilling it, to investigate a topic or develop a project. Successful completion of the designated tasks may require skills of concentration, patience, creativity, diligence, persistence, and maturity. Successful completion reflects the young girl's readiness for womanhood. Some initiations even include creative ways to symbolize the death-rebirth process, such as requiring initiates to go through a tunnel of cloth (symbolizing the birth canal) or passing under a bridge made of the upraised arms of the elder women of the community.

In the final, postliminal phase of the initiation process, the young woman may have new clothes or be given a new name. She will often display new skills (such as Afua and her agemates, who danced and sang after their initiation), make presentations, or reflect on her new knowledge and understanding of what it means to be a woman. Her reintroduction into the community will be festive, a celebration of the success that is not only hers but also that of all the women who have preceded her, as she is welcomed as a new, creative, powerful force in the universe.

• • •

Many cultures and societies have long understood the importance of preparing their girls to become women who know how to express their soul's beauty, creativity, and purpose. They have done this through rites of passage and initiation processes. Unfortunately, most women in Western cultures have not gone through a formal initiation process to mark their transition from childhood to womanhood. This has sometimes been due to the fear of women's power or the misunderstanding of the meaning and role of the rituals used in initiation. However, this situation is beginning to change as more women are coming to see the value of this type of ritual and ceremony.

Perhaps you would like to get together with friends and important adult women in your life to develop an initiation ceremony for yourself. What follows is a series of pointers to help you fashion an initiation to fit your needs. And remember, although this book is for young girls, the following ideas can be used by "girls" of any age who want to honor themselves as women.

- Identify the purpose, goals, and objectives for your initiation. Do you want to honor the beginning of menstruation (rather than curse it)? The onset of puberty? You may want to celebrate the natural cycles associated with being female. Develop a statement of purpose to help guide you as you develop your initiation process.

- Identify the adult women who can coordinate the activities related to the initiation ceremony. Although your input as an initiate will be important, it will be the elder women (your mother, female relatives, and/or mentors) who will be responsible for your training: developing the classes, projects, and experiences to reinforce the values connected to your statement of purpose. Seek out women you know and admire whom you feel can be supportive and affirming of you in your growth into womanhood. They can familiarize themselves with rites of passage programs and initiation ceremonies using the various community and written resources available. It would be great to find adult women who have been through the process themselves. Ask around.

- Organize the rites of passage and initiation process. How long will the preparation take? What types of challenges or ordeals will you have to face? What will your re-entry into the community look like? Although some people do ritual as part of a shortened initiation process (several hours or day-long), the true spirit of initiation occurs as part of the longer rites of passage process, to provide for the training in various educational areas. Depending on your statement of purpose, you might want to cover several or all of the following components: family history, sex education, spirituality, community, physical health, emotional health, interpersonal relationships, assertiveness/leadership, values clarification, goal setting, and creativity.

Consequently, the actual rites of passage process (preparation, initiation, and ceremony) may be days, weeks, or months long. It will be useful to develop a schedule of activities, and identify resource people to help with the implementation of the process. Again, much of this work may be handled by the elder women, with your input.

- Develop rituals and determine ritual setting, time, objects, sound, etc. This is the really fun part! Choose a space that will allow you to do your activities freely and comfortably. Because of the sacred nature of what you will be doing during the actual initiation activities, you will not want to be interrupted by telephones, pagers, or other types of devices. The time of day and year are also considerations for your planning. Again, you can refer to your statement of purpose to inform your decision-making around this issue. You may want to include music, poetry, or prose that addresses the theme of womanhood. You might also include objects of personal relevance in your initiation (like clothing or keepsakes from an admired or influential woman in your life) that represent positive and powerful aspects of womanhood to discuss and share. Remember, you can be creative about the when, where, what, and how of your initiation. Use your imagination and work with your elders!

- Develop and identify a challenge or a series of challenges that must be met as proof of your readiness for womanhood. This could take on many forms: memorizing passages that speak to the experiences of womanhood, practice of adult activities, activities that require individual concentration, persistence, and commitment, activities that require group cooperation and/or collaboration, etc. The challenge(s) could be something that occurs on the actual day of the initiation ceremony or it could be something that is to be completed beforehand and presented on that day. The challenge should not be something that puts you in danger (such as hazing), but something that helps you become more mindful and conscious of your new status as a woman. While the designated challenge(s) can be developed with your input, it is most often the case that the elders will also develop some challenge(s) that will be unknown to you until the actual day of the ceremony. This will add to the mystery of the event and make the achievement even that much more memorable and meaningful!

• Develop ritual(s) to reinforce the successful mastery of the challenge. One example of a ritual that can be used after the symbolic rebirth requires you and other initiates to stand in front of a mirror, stating the following affirmation: "I am a daughter of women. It is right and good that I am a woman; I honor my experience and will tell you my story" (adapted from Patricia Lynn Reilly).

• Plan who and how others will be involved in the celebration after the initiation ceremony. Although women generally take responsibility for the preparation phase and the initiation itself, some postliminal phases have included men from the community. Again, this decision can be informed by your purpose and goals. Food, drink, singing, dancing, even storytelling might be a part of the celebration after initiation. Organize this so that it reflects your energy and spirit.

• Finally, party and enjoy being a young woman!

• • •

# Appendix II
# Maiden/Mother MoonCircles

## Penny Andrews

> Penny Andrews, an interfaith minister and chaplain, offers groups for women from nine to ninety exploring the sacred through creativity. She founded the MinGei (Japanese for "art of the people") Center for Interfaith Spirituality in Cottage Grove, Wisconsin. Her doctoral project, ElderSpirit Speaks, is in process with the University of Creation Spirituality. Contact her at pandrews@chorus.net.

All things are built one stone at a time, and so it was with the Maiden/ Mother MoonCircle.

In 1992, I was a woman in my early forties when I gave birth to my daughter, Amelia Rose. I had prayed for a girl and waited over twenty years for my second child to be born. She was my dream come true. But Amelia was not born into a world that was particularly user-friendly to girls and women. I knew this through my years of various kinds of glass ceilings, the failure to pass the ERA, the continued violence and abuse globally and locally of women, and the pervasive, gnawing depression in women I could see everywhere. How could I raise Amelia to know a wide-open terrain of possibility with a limitless sky?

During Amelia's toddler years, the powerful work by Mary Pipher, *Reviving Ophelia*, had been published; the studies documenting adolescent girls' plummeting self-esteem were often in the newspaper; and the statistics on teachers responding to boys more frequently than girls in the classroom was on my mind, as was the continued use of underdeveloped women's bodies in magazines, commercials, and elsewhere in the media. What could a mother do to help her child through obvious pitfalls that would face her? It is a dilemma all mothers face.

Blessedly, at the same time, I had ventured into women's spirituality groups. There I found some of the answers to how to address these difficult challenges. Being in a women's group where we spoke our truths and shared deeply with each other of our joys and sorrows, walking into a room with 300 women drumming and chanting would be two of the most powerful spiritual experiences of my life. To this day, it is the marker for me of ecstatic communion with the divine.

Learning about the sacred feminine from India, Africa, Ireland, Greece, Japan, China, the Native American tradition, the cross-cultural and mysterious Black Madonna, and the groundbreaking work of Marija Gimbutas (see the further reading section) forever changed the face of the divine for me. It became clear to me that girls from our culture who have a monotheistic view of a God who is always described as "He" must struggle much harder to find the "God within" than their male counterparts, who can identify with "Him."

This was too low a ceiling for Amelia and, I began to realize, for all girls. Only the ends of the universe would do for our girls. What could I do?

I had studied and taught the "Rise Up and Call Her Name" curriculum of the Unitarian Universalist Church—a multifaceted, interfaith approach to learning about goddesses from around the world—but it was clearly written for adults. So, I asked myself, how could a circle be created that would make a girl feel comfortable to learn material not taught anywhere else?

I began to reflect about myself as a child. Clearly, in my prepubescent years, my mother had been my best friend. Who better than one's mother to enter into circle with? And so the Maiden/Mother MoonCircle was born.

One of my teachers, Yoruban priestess Luisah Teish, speaks strongly of how important it is for girls to experience ritual. It is a thirst we all have, and girls have it even more profoundly as they approach the time of puberty, for the transition from girl to woman brings with it so much internal change. One of the ways to create a safe framework for this rite of passage is in community with others who have experienced the same changes and peers facing these same changes.

# The Circle Center

Every month the altar, placed on the middle of the floor, expresses some of the intention of the evening. It does not take elaborate items to create an aesthetic resonance. Simple natural items like leaves, a branch, nuts, or grasses are quite powerful. Also, when possible, I bring in a small statue of the goddess we will spend time with that evening. Daughters and mothers are encouraged to bring in their own altar objects as well.

# Themes

The themes are based on inspiration and season. For instance, one month I was giving a talk to a women's spirituality group on the Black Madonna and had collected images and material I wanted to share. Coincidentally, one of the mothers of our group had just returned from a pilgrimage to southern France to study the Black Madonna. Another month, I had spent time studying Jewish ritual, and the next MoonCircle fell on Brigid's Day, a combination that gave birth to Brigid's *tisch* (see page 208). I often rely on synchronicity to assist in theme selection, and I am never sorry.

# The Opening Ritual

We gather outside the meeting room, and there we follow a tradition taught to me by Luisah Teish. We chant a song the women in a Nigerian village sing as they are coming together, one that not only calls the women and girls to come, but the spirits of those invited women who cannot. It goes: "Ee Lay Mah Dah Lay Me Oh, Ee Lay Mah Dah Lay Me Oh." Any chant will do, but there is something magical in using sounds that are unfamiliar but whose meaning is clear.

As we stand in a line waiting to enter the room, one of the women uses a mister to spray around the woman or girl's body front and back before she enters the room. Then, very purposefully, leading with her left foot, the girl enters and the next person is sprayed. Luisah Teish would use a lovely jasmine scent; I chose to use 4711, a cologne made in Germany that my grandmother used to wear. Engaging the sense of smell is very important in ritual, for it is one of our strongest senses and can assist in the delineation between the experience being in "ordinary" reality and one that is sacred.

The purpose of misting is to cleanse the aura—to leave cares, worries, and challenges of the world behind as one enters into sacred space. Whether done with the smoke of sage, a feather gently brushing all around, a bell, or any other number of other ways, the intention is the same. One's energy is separated from the outside world as she enters sacred space.

The opening of the chant and the misting is done every time we come together. It becomes something to be counted on, which the girls know and appreciate. The mist is soothing even in the middle of winter. We laugh when someone's glasses get sprayed accidentally while someone else is being misted. This community-building ritual sets a joyful tone. The misting brings mothers and daughters out of their being a pair and into the larger circle.

## Toning

We begin our circle with toning, which brings the circle together on the same wavelength. We used the simple toning of "MA," which brings in energy from above and grounds it in the group. The sound "Mm" is for the divine and brings energy from above to earth, and "Ah" is the sound used for the heart chakra. We chant this three times. The shift in group energy is palpable. It is delicious.

## The Touch-In or Check-In

We begin this by stating our name and then our motherline. This extremely powerful exercise has become part of our regular gathering ritual. We say the names of all the women from whom we descend. For instance, "I am Penny, daughter of Hildegarde, daughter of Anna, daughter of Maria." Doing this has a profound effect on the mothers and gives the girls a very concrete sense of lineage. One of the mothers whose family had been Mormon researched her genealogical records and was able to trace three additional generations of women and learn of some of the struggles her women ancestors had faced with polygamy and the difficulty that pioneering entailed. Her eleven-year-old daughter listened to this story, learning a historical family story and perhaps gaining some insight about a difficult situation with her maternal grandmother. Another mother joyfully reported a conversation she had had with her mother about their lineage and was also able to add three generations of women.

A few years back I spoke to an elderly uncle who is the family historian in England about our family line, and he told many stories about the family—but because of this heightened awareness I had from doing this exercise, it became clear he was not telling the women's stories. After a couple of promptings in which I asked him to specifically speak about the women, I was able to get to the stories of their lives. They were rich indeed.

Often the girls follow their mothers in speaking the motherline and in so doing get a prompting to remember. As a child, I remember wondering about the male lineage of the Bible and the monarchies of Europe, wondering where the women were. The girls of the MoonCircle will always have another context for this experience. This simple activity is highly transformational.

After speaking the motherline, we speak about whatever is important to us. We sometimes use nonverbal check-ins as well, using hand gestures to describe what we are feeling. A rapid, jerky movement might imply "busy," moving too fast; a wavelike gesture might mean things were going smoothly; wild gestures could suggest "chaos alert." These are fun to do and keep us in our bodies. This culture relies on our heads to do the majority of our activities, so it is essential to share how our bodies can be brought into our sense of spiritual aliveness also.

There is a lovely concept called the Body Prayer that involves the whole self in celebrating life. The Sun Salutation from yoga is one form, but there are many others. Here is one I find transformational:

### Body Prayer

1. Hands on your heart, take a couple of centering breaths.

2. Raise your open arms to the sky with face looking up.

3.     Bring your hands back to your heart.

4.     Touch the ground below you.

5.     Standing up, put your hands back on your heart.

6.     Slowly, with your left hand over your heart and your right arm outstretched at a 90-degree angle from your side, with your face looking to the right, begin to turn your body in a full circle.

7.     Repeat this several times.

To offer young women and their mothers time in their bodies together that is sublimely pleasurable and deep is something rare in this culture indeed. Drumming, dancing, and singing can all be integrated into the MoonCircle and provide a playful, creative, and honest way to be together, celebrating the spirit in our lives.

## Synchronicities

In the altar space, we often place some form of divination tool. We used a wide variety: cards, runes, stones, and I Ching sticks, to name a few.  We then select something to represent our spiritual state. The idea is to integrate the synchronicity of the tool. Each person is left to their own interpretation of how their particular selection fits their lives.

Synchronicity, serendipity, flow, and grace all have a similar meaning and each of these calls on our deeper self to form the meaningful pattern. Members of the MoonCircle community are often surprised at the relevance their selection has to their lives. Being guided from within is a lifelong skill that needs to be formed and validated; in this circle, we support each other's learning.

During this part of the evening, the group occasionally shares dreams. The girls absolutely love sharing dreams. When we do dream interpretation, we share ideas by saying, "If this were my dream . . ." and then only speaking "I" statements. (As an example, "If this were my dream, I would wonder why the sled I was riding on was floating on water.") We also recognize that our dreams are messages from the soul.

# Teachings

When I began learning about the divine feminine, I strongly believed in the sacredness of the Earth and was committed to a practice that honored Mother Earth. And I began to learn from the various cultures of goddesses who blurred the line between Earth and deity. Learning of Marija Gimbutus' work, watching the Canadian video series *The Burning Times*, studying the patriarchy and the ways in which various traditions today do not allow women to claim their own religious authority, I came to see how essential it is for women to reclaim their spiritual authority not only for ourselves but for the future of the planet.

The divine feminine IS an Earth-centered tradition. There is no celebration of her in her many guises that does not encompass love and devotion to the Earth and all her creatures. As girls learn of the sacredness of all life, they begin to understand the sacredness of their life and the life that is all around them. This life-affirming philosophy is core to our future. The girls of today must not be stopped by society's flagrant exploitation of women, and one very powerful way to begin to do this is through the deep understanding of the sacred feminine and its mirror of the divine within us. Our girls need to know about goddesses, not necessarily to become worshippers but to know that aspects of womanhood are to be honored. Whether it is the power of Kali, the compassion of Kuan Yin, the brightness of Amaterasu, or the earthiness of the Black Madonna, these images of the divine expand our understanding of our own truth. The Venus of Willendorf, the Aeschulian Goddess, and the Goddess of Lespugue all teach us how ancient the sacredness of women is. We cannot so easily diminish ourselves when we recognize women's divinity.

Teaching about the sacred feminine also prompts the question, "Where are the women of my tradition?" This question creates a whole new aspect of the spiritual path, and this begins the journey all of us take in finding what is true and meaningful for us. It opens us to explore the history of our faith and ethnic traditions and what is essential for us to create a real spiritual path that honors our womanhood.

# Creativity

Our group culminates by spending time with our creativity. It is a lifelong friend and holds the key to vitality, healing, and life with purpose. In the MoonCircle, it takes on many forms. In my experience working with women, open a box of art supplies and magic happens. Women are destined to create, whether in the literal sense or in the heightened use of our dominant right brain. In creativity, we come alive.

This aspect of the MoonCircle has always been the favorite. Whether working with mandalas, labyrinths, clay, poems, cloth, song, paintings, beads, or any other medium, girls and mothers are on equal ground. Engaging the the birthright of creativity, this brings forward joy, surprise, and learning.

One evening around February 1, our theme was Brigid's Tisch, in which we melded the Jewish idea of tisch with the celebration of Brigid's Day. The teaching that evening was on Brigid. I spoke of her role as a major deity of the Celts, whose popularity was so strong that she became the most popular saint of the Celts when Catholicism was introduced in Ireland. She was the Celtic triple goddess, dark mother, nature goddess, or lover/sister/virgin. She ruled poetry, inspiration, smithcraft, divination, and was the protectress of women, animals, and cooking. Her totem animal was the magical cow. The teaching ended with the beautiful metaphorical image of Brigid hanging her cloak on the rays of the sun.

A tisch involves sitting around the kitchen table on the Jewish Sabbath and singing *niguns* (wordless Jewish songs) and sharing poems and stories as one eats challah bread and drinks wine. One of the mothers who had been raised Jewish brought in some exquisite challah she had made for the celebration, while I brought in an exotic-tasting juice. Our project for that evening was to write a poem to tie in with Brigid's domain. I asked everyone to write out six words about anything. These were written on six separate sheets that were then shuffled and redistributed, with everyone keeping one of her own words, the one she was particularly drawn to. From a basket containing the remaining words, we each pulled five words to be incorporated into a poem with the one word we had saved.

When we had completed writing our poems, we began to sing and eat. The song uses simple syllables like "by-dy-dy, dy, dee, di," and is typically sung in a minor key. This melody became the theme between storytelling and poem sharing. Members took turns sharing their poems and telling stories that evoked family and spirit. The following poem, written by a nine-year-old member of the circle, stands out from this evening.

> *We are all Feminine, together.*
> *We may be full of anger,*
> *We may be full of secrets,*
> *We may feel fresh as fruit,*
> *We may feel a sense of new life,*
> *We may feel comfy,*
> *We may all feel different from one another,*
> *But we are all here together*
> *Like one full moon.*
> —Ali Yoder, aged 9

Creativity is our light in the dark times, a roadmap when we are lost. It is imperative our girls are given this piece of information. It serves us personally, and it serves our universe also. We were never meant to become rutted in a small, narrow path. The universe is constantly creating and so are we, as beings born of this universe. When women were made small from patriarchy, our gifts of creativity were also made small. The line "anonymous was a woman" is one of the saddest and most telling of this truth.

In my darkest times, it is to my creativity I have gone to be uplifted, guided, and to seek new ways of being on this journey. With a Prozac culture, with the increasing complexity of social ills, with our own burning desire for aliveness, it is to our creativity we can turn for new and inspired answers. Our young women need to make friends with this aspect of their divinity, with the divine spark within them. The future depends on the voices of women adding their song to the choir.

## Our Elders

A couple of months after starting the MoonCircle, I ran into a friend, Barbara, a woman in her late seventies who is still actively on her spiritual journey. Barbara's openness to the journey and to sharing her accumulated wisdom are evident in conversation. Her eyes twinkle and her physical presence is strong and warm. I remembered, from working with Luisah Teish, the village's important role for an elder. When there is a dispute or decision to be made, the elder's opinion is always sought. I asked the women of the MoonCircle if they would consider having an elder join us, and unanimously, they approved. Barbara, delighted to be asked, joined us the next circle.

Because of the diffused geography of families today, grandmothers are not as present as they used to be. When Barbara joined us she began to fulfill the role of unconditional acceptance for mothers and daughters alike. She offered her perspective freely, participated enthusiastically in the creative endeavors, and loved sharing her stories and taking part in the rituals.

Something else happened, though, as our circle came to rely on Barbara for her wisdom and love. I received this e-mail: "Thank you so much for including me in the MoonCircle. Beautiful experience, beautiful people. It could change my life. —Barbara." Barbara, an academic and social activist, spent little time in her youth with her creativity; every time she took a risk with her creativity in the MoonCircle, she fell in love. Today, nearing her eightieth birthday, she is taking creative writing classes and is looking forward to some art courses in the spring.

Is it the Circle with women of all ages that invokes transformation? Did our times together bring forward something ancient and deep? I believe it did.

# Closings

It is important to have a closing ritual. We varied ours with songs, hand-holding, and blessings. We pray in the circle for healing, guidance, truth, beauty, and to reinforce spiritual values that need to be expressed out loud for our girls, and for the girls to hear their own voices lifted up.

# The Power of a Blessing

What if every family blessed each other during sad times and happy times? What if our children grew up knowing what it is like to be touched, acknowledged, and feeling part of a chain of blessings that extends far out into the universe and deep into the Earth's core? What if our mothers knew their energies were moving life into the future? What if they knew their daughter's love, simply stated in a circle of women, witnessed and acknowledged respectfully? What if our elders knew the gentle blessings they bestow to those they touch—to their families? What if we touched each other with our words, our hearts, our wishes, just so? Wouldn't we feel that much more heard, that much more loved, that much more alive, that much more at one with spirit? When we bless, we pray; when we pray, we are in communion; and when we are in communion, we create a green and growing place in our heart.

The idea of the Maiden/Mother MoonCircle is ancient. In our time together, we tap into the wise woman, wild child, and mother in each of us. This circle works because we are women coming together on an elemental level. Ritual, exploring the sacred feminine, and time with our creativity are taproots that each of us has embedded within on a cellular level. It is time to reclaim this taproot. Let it take form and live again. Let mothers, daughters, and grandmothers celebrate womanhood in circle together, sharing the mysteries, joys, and sorrows of living in a sacred way, and letting our life live through us as it has always meant to be. We need but remember, and remember to remember.

# Further Reading

## *Books, nonfiction*

Adler, Margot. *Drawing Down the Moon*. Beacon, 1997.

Allen, Paula Gunn. *Grandmothers of the Light: A Medicine Woman's Sourcebook*. Beacon, 1992.

Ardinger, Barbara. *Goddess Meditations*. Llewellyn, 1998.

Budapest, Zsuzsanna E. *The Grandmother of Time: A Women's Book of Celebrations, Spells and Sacred Objects for Every Month of the Year*. HarperSanFrancisco, 1989.

Carnes, R. & S. Craig. *Sacred Circles*. HarperSanFrancisco, 1998.

Castillo, Ana, editor. *Goddess of the Americas*. Riverhead, 1997.

Downing, Christine. *The Goddess*. Continuum, 1996.

Ellis, Normandi. *Dreams of Isis: A Woman's Spiritual Sojourn*. Quest Books, 1995.

Galland, China. *Longing for Darkness: Tara and the Black Madonna*. Viking, 1990.

Gimbutas, Marija. *The Language of the Goddess*. HarperSanFrancisco, 1991.

Grace, Patricia. *Wahine Toa: Women of Maori Myth*. Paintings and drawings by Robyn Kahukiwa. Collins, 1984.

Grimm, John and Jacob. *The Complete Grimm's Fairy Tales*. Pantheon, 1944.

Husain, Shahrukh. *The Goddess: An Illustrated Guide to the Divine Feminine*. One Spirit, 1997.

Jade. *To Know: A Guide to Women's Magic and Spirituality*. Delphi Press, 1991.

Johnson, Buffie. *Lady of the Beasts: Ancient Images of the Goddess and her Sacred Animals*. Harper & Row, 1988.

Lonnrot, Elias. *The Kalevala*. Keither Bosley, translator. Oxford University Press, 1999.

Matthews, Caitlin. *Elements of the Goddess*. Element, 1997.

Middleton, Julie Forest. *Songs for Earthlings*. Emerald Earth Publishing, 1998.

Monaghan, Patricia. *The Goddess Path*. Llewellyn, 1999.

——. *The Goddess Companion*. Llewellyn, 1999.

——. *The New Book of Goddesses and Heroines*. Llewellyn, 1997.

——. *O Mother Sun: A New View of the Cosmic Feminine*. Crossing Press, 1994.

Moore, M., G. Gilyard, K. King, & N. Warfield-Coppock. *Transformation, A Rite of Passage Manual for African-American Girls*. Stars Press, 1987.

Morrison, Dorothy. *Everyday Magic*. Llewellyn, 1998.

Muten, Burleigh. *Return of the Great Goddess*. Shambala, 1998.

——, editor. *Her Words: An Anthology of Poetry About the Great Goddess*. Shambhala, 1999.

Onassis, Jacqueline, editor. *The Firebird and Other Russian Fairy Tales*. The Viking Press, 1978.

RavenWolf, Silver. *Teen Witch*. Llewellyn, 1997.

Some, M. *The Healing Wisdom of Africa*. Tarcher/Putnam, 1977.

Starck, M. (1993). *Women's Medicine Ways: Cross-cultural Rites of Passage*. Crossing Press, 1993.

Starhawk. *The Spiral Dance: A Rebirth of the Ancient Religion of the Great Goddess*. Harper & Row, 1979.

Stone, Merlin. *When God Was A Woman*. Harcourt Brace Jovanovich, 1976.

Teish, Luisah. *Jambalaya: The Natural Woman's Books of Personal Charms and Practical Rituals*. Harper & Row, 1985.

Waldherr, Kris. *Embracing the Goddess Within*. Beyond Words, 1997.

## Books, fiction

Bierhorst, John. *The Woman Who Fell From the Sky*. William Morrow, 1993.

Block, Francesca Lia. *Girl Goddess* (series). HarperCollins Juvenile, 1996.

Cunningham, Elizabeth. *The Wild Mother*. Station Hill Press, 1993.

———. *Daughter of the Shining Isles*. Station Hill Press, 2000.

———. *How to Spin Gold, A Woman's Tale*. Station Hill Press, 1997.

Cruz Martinze, Alejandro. *The Woman Who Outshone the Sun/La Mujer Que Brillaba Aun Mas Que El Sol*. Children's Book Press, 1984.

George, Jean Craighead. *The Talking Earth*. Harper Trophy, 1987.

Hamilton, Virginia. *Her Stories: African-American Folktales, Fairy Tales and True Tales*. Scholastic Trade, 1995.

LeGuin, Ursula. *Wizard of Earthsea*. Bantam Spectra, 1984.

Llywelyn, Morgan. *The Horse Goddess*. Tor, 1998.

Masters, Alexis. *The Guiliana Legacy*. HCI, 2000.

McDonald, George. *At the Back of the North Wind*. Bridge-Logos, 1998.

Cooper, Susan. *The Dark Is Rising*. Aladdin, 1986.

McKillip, Patricia. *Forgotten Beasts of Eld*. Harcourt Brace, 1996.

Miles, Miska. *Annie and the Old One*. Little, Brown & Co., 1985.

Reed-Jones, Carol. *The Tree in the Ancient Forest*. Dawn Publications, 1995.

Wood, Audrey. *Rainbow Bridge*. Doubleday, 1996.

## *Magazines*

*Beltane Papers,* quarterly magazine, P.O. Box 29694, Bellingham, WA 98228-1694.

*Sagewoman,* quarterly magazine. P.O. Box 641, Point Arena, CA 95468.
www.sagewoman.com

*Of a Like Mind,* quarterly newsletter, P.O. Box 644, Madison, WI 53716.

*Goddessing Regenerated,* newsletter, P.O. Box 269, Valrico, FL 33595.

*New Moon Magazine.* P.O. Box 3626, Duluth, MN 55803.
www.newmoon.org

*Teen Voices* ℅ Women Express, P.O. Box 120-027, Boston, MA 02112-0027.
www.teenvoices.com

# National Hotlines

Reprinted with kind permission by Silver RavenWolf from *Witches' Night Out* (Llewellyn, 2000).

## Alcohol and Drug Abuse

Al-Anon & Alateen: 1-800-356-9996
National Clearinghouse for Alcohol & Drug Information: 1-800-SAY-NOTO
National Cocaine Hotline: 1-800-262-2463
Alcohol & Drug Dependency Hopeline: 1-800-622-2255
National Institute on Drug Abuse Hotline: 1-800-622-HELP
Mothers Against Drunk Driving: 1-800-438-MADD

## Abuse

Bureau of Indian Affairs Child Abuse Hotline: 1-800-633-5133
Boy's Town: 1-800-448-3000
Child Help USA: 1-800-422-4453
National Respite Locaters Service: 1-800-773-5433
National Domestic Violence Hotline: 1-800-799-7233
National Clearinghouse of Child Abuse and Neglect: 1-800-394-3366
National Resource Center on Domestic Violence: 1-800-553-2508
Rape, Abuse & Incest National Network: 1-800-656-4673
Resource Center on Domestic Violence, Child Protection and Custody: 1-800-527-3223

## Runaway Hotlines

Covenant House Nineline: 1-800-999-9999
National Runaway Switchboard: 1-800-621-4000

## National Child Welfare

Child Find of America: 1-800-I-AM-LOST
Child Quest International Sighting Line: 1-800-248-8020
National Referral Network for Kids in Crisis: 1-800-KID-SAVE

## Health & AIDS/HIV

AIDS Helpline: 1-800-548-4659
Ask A Nurse Connection: 1-800-535-1111
National AIDS Hotline: 1-800-342-AIDS
STD National Hotline: 1-800-227-8922

# Index

# REACH FOR THE MOON

*Llewellyn publishes hundreds of books on your favorite subjects!*
*To get these exciting books, including the ones on the following pages,*
*check your local bookstore or order them directly from Llewellyn.*

### Order by Phone
- Call toll-free within the U.S. and Canada, 1-800-THE MOON
- In Minnesota, call (651) 291-1970
- We accept VISA, MasterCard, and American Express

### Order by Mail
- Send the full price of your order (MN residents add 7% sales tax) in U.S. funds, plus postage & handling to:

  **Llewellyn Worldwide**
  **P.O. Box 64383, Dept. 1-56718-442-1**
  **St. Paul, MN 55164–0383, U.S.A.**

### Postage & Handling
(For the U.S., Canada, and Mexico)
- $4.00 for orders $15.00 and under
- $5.00 for orders over $15.00
- No charge for orders over $100.00

We ship UPS in the continental United States. We ship standard mail to P.O. boxes. Orders shipped to Alaska, Hawaii, the Virgin Islands, and Puerto Rico are sent first-class mail. Orders shipped to Canada and Mexico are sent surface mail.

**International orders:** Airmail—add freight equal to price of each book to the total price of order, plus $5.00 for each non-book item (audio tapes, etc.).

**Surface mail**—Add $1.00 per item.

*Allow 2 weeks for delivery on all orders.*
*Postage and handling rates subject to change.*

### Discounts
We offer a 20% discount to group leaders or agents. You must order a minimum of 5 copies of the same book to get our special quantity price.

### Free Catalog
Get a free copy of our color catalog, *New Worlds of Mind and Spirit.* Subscribe for just $10.00 in the United States and Canada ($30.00 overseas, airmail). Many bookstores carry *New Worlds*—ask for it!

**Visit our website at www.llewellyn.com for more information.**

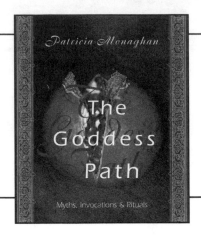

# The Goddess Companion
## Daily Meditations on the Feminine Spirit

## PATRICIA MONAGHAN

Engage your feminine spirit each day of the year! Here are hundreds of authentic goddess prayers, invocations, chants, and songs—one for each day of the year. They come from dozens of sources, ranging from the great classical European authors Ovid and Horace, to the marvelously passionate Hindu poets Ramprasad and Ramakrishna, to the anonymous gifted poets who first composed the folksongs of Lithuania, West Africa, and Alaska. In fresh, contemporary language that maintains the spirit of the originals, these prayers can be used for personal meditation, for private or public ritual, or for your own creative inspiration. They capture the depth of feeling, the philosophical complexity, and the ecological awareness of goddess cultures the world over.

Organized as a daily meditation book, *The Goddess Companion* is also indexed by culture, goddess, and subject, so you can easily find prayers for specific purposes. Following each prayer is a thoughtfully written piece of prose by Patricia Monaghan which illustrates the aspects of the Goddess working in our everyday lives.

- A perpetual calendar with a daily reading on each page—366 in all
- Includes prayers from Greece, Rome, North and South America, Lithuania, Latvia, Japan, Finland, Scandinavia, India, and many others
- In translations that fully reveal their beauty, making them immediately accessible and emotionally powerful
- Locate goddess prayers by culture, subject, and goddess names

1-56718-463-4
312 pp., 7½ x 9⅛                                                                    $17.95

## To order, call 1-800-THE MOON
Prices subject to change without notice

## The New Book of Goddesses & Heroines
### Patricia Monaghan

They come out in your dreams, your creativity, your passion, and in all of your relationships. They represent you in all your glory and complexity, and you represent them. They are the goddesses and heroines that form our true history—your history. Let these mythic stories nourish your soul as they speak to you on a level as deep and mysterious as the source of life itself.

The third edition of this classic reference offers a complete, shining collection of goddess myths from around the globe. Discover more than 1,500 goddesses in Australia, Africa, North and South America, Asia, Europe—and experience her as she truly is. This new edition also adds hundreds of new entries to the original text—information found only in rare or limited editions and obscure sources.

There is a new section on "Cultures of the Goddess," which provides the location, time, and general features of the major religious system detailed in the myths. A comprehensive index, titled "Names of the Goddess," provides all available names, with variants. Stories, rites, invocations, and prayers are recorded in the "Myths" section, as well as a list of common symbols. Never before has such a vast panorama of female divinity been recorded in one source.

1-56718-465-0
384 pp., 8½ x 11, illus., photos                                    $19.95

## To order, call 1-800-THE MOON
Prices subject to change without notice